Foreword by Steve Gallagher

D[]LETE

Ridding your life of pornography God's way

Dustin Renz

DELETE

Dustin Renz

MAKE WAY MINISTRIES

For more information, please contact MAKE WAY MINISTRIES online at: www.makewayministries.com

Library of Congress Control Number: 2025903846
Renz, Dustin 1983-
Delete: Ridding Your Life of Pornography God's Way
First Edition: April 2025
Make Way Ministries

ISBN: 979-8-9927563-0-2

Printed in the United States of America.
10 9 8 7 6 5 4 3 2 1

OTHER TRANSLATIONS AND PARAPHRASES USED
(in order of appearance)

ACKNOWLEDGMENTS

I want to express my sincere gratitude for the contributions of several people who helped bring this project to completion:

Thank you to my wife, Brittany. First, I am so grateful that you stood by my side through my personal journey into freedom. Second, thank you for the time you invested in editing the book and providing important feedback.

Thank you to Nate Danser, Scott Wilson and Sean Ardizzone, for examining the manuscript and giving helpful insight based on your areas of expertise.

Thank you to Shy Renz, for helping to proofread the manuscript and for your encouragement along the way.

Thank you to Steve Gallagher, for your valuable feedback on the writing of this book.

Thank you to Jonathan Willetts, for an amazing cover. Your time and skill are greatly appreciated.

I am so grateful to each of you for helping this book become better than I could have made it on my own. May the Lord bless you richly for your time and sacrifice.

DEDICATION

I dedicate this book to the men who will read its contents and put the principles into practice. My heart is rejoicing in advance because I am already praying for you and I know the Lord is going to do a great work in your life. Although your story up to this point may be one of frustration and failure, may it soon become one of faithfulness and fruitfulness.

TABLE OF CONTENTS

FOREWORD

I assume you are reading this book because you have been viewing pornography, maybe even become addicted to it. No doubt you're wondering how this happened to you. I think I can help you understand.

Let's begin with the porn industry that is behind those websites you've been visiting. You need to understand that this entire field of commerce is controlled by powerful demon entities. The producers, actors and promoters involved are all inspired by the enemy in their work. The evil men and demonic forces at work there are determined to lead you into an ever greater bondage. They want to own you for the rest of your life. That's how this industry thrives and how the enemy destroys lives.

One day you had your first encounter with this horrid business. You will probably never forget what you experienced when you saw your first pornographic video. I'm sure it was as if something exploded inside you. You were instantly hooked. You returned to that sewer time after time in the following days.

To find your way out of this nasty addiction, you must first understand what happened to you. The human brain contains a mass of interconnecting nerves. Impulses travel through those nerves with every thought and action. Repeating behavior creates a highway through that nervous system.

A good way to think of it is a field full of weeds and brush lying between two villages. Over time, people walking back and forth between these villages develop a trail that becomes wider, smoother and easier to walk on. That is how the Lord created the human being's ability to form a habit: Do something repeatedly and it becomes increasingly easier to continue doing it.

When the activity is pleasurable an addiction can easily become established. This occurs with the help of a human hormone called dopamine, also known as the pleasure hormone. Think about the first time you viewed pornography. That sense of exhilaration you experienced occurred because dopamine flooded your system, giving you a sense of tremendous euphoria.

However, each time a person experiences a particular pleasure, less dopamine is released and the sense of euphoria diminishes. Over time, the thrill wanes and all that is left is a demanding addiction.

As if that wasn't enough to have to deal with, you must also consider the spiritual bondage that has set in. You were just trying to have a little fun by looking at some images and videos. You didn't realize that you were spiritually connecting with unclean spirits that were busy establishing a stronghold in your inner man.

Humans are spiritual beings and everything we do has spiritual implications. As a young guy begins making forays into demonically controlled websites, he will increasingly come under the power of their spiritual darkness. The Bible uses the term idolatry to describe this phenomenon.

God created us with the capacity to love. This is why the greatest commandment is that we love God with all our heart, soul and mind. Believers can and should love God with that kind of intensity and commitment. If we don't, it's probably because we've allowed something else to become the primary object of our affections.

Millions of people are addicted to various forms of pleasure. Many of us have given our hearts over to the pursuit of illicit sex. The thought of it is so delicious that we could easily spend hours fantasizing about it. Other people become addicted to the high they receive when they use drugs or consume alcohol. Still others love food so much that they regularly overeat. Or think about Scrooge's obsession with money. The Bible calls the desire that drives people toward their particular form of sin "the lust of the flesh."

The more a person indulges their particular vice, the stronger the bondage to it becomes. The love they should have for God is being spent on their beloved idol. Little by little, they come under the power of the enemy.

So that, in a nutshell, is how an addiction to pornography is formed and strengthened. I would guess that you are already experiencing what I'm referring to at some level.

Look, if you have dug yourself into a pit of darkness, don't despair! The good news is that the Lord has provided a means of escape. Dustin has learned from his own painful experience, not only the addictive nature of pornography, but also how to break the hold of it.

This book provides you with the pathway into freedom he took years ago. Carefully read every chapter because each one is loaded with God's wisdom on how to turn your life around. The Lord has made a way out for you. All you have to do is follow those steps and you too can come into a life of freedom.

Steve Gallagher,
Founder, Pure Life Ministries

Intro

Start:// the-journey-begins

I WAS FACILITATING A MEN'S BIBLE STUDY recently and we were discussing the topic of our secret thought lives. As might be expected, a large part of that conversation revolved around sexual purity. As we talked about the extensive damage that pornography is causing in the lives of men in the church, the thought came to me: "Pornography is possibly the most wicked sin to ever enter the human race." It was at that moment I felt the inspiration to write this book.

My own experience has created a passion in me to see men get free. As I thought about the prospects of writing on this topic, my mind went to the many men that I have counseled over the last few years who are walking in freedom today. I reflected upon the process that the Lord used to set me free from porn when I was a student in Pure Life Ministries in 2011. My mind also went back to the many years that I squandered with the talons of sexual sin deeply embedded in my heart. I concluded that I owe it to the Christian community to take everything I have learned and put it into book form.

Unfortunately, the contents of *Delete* are desperately needed by the church community of our day. In fact, within the last twenty-four hours of writing these words, a ministry couple whose lives had been shattered due to the husband's hidden sexual sin reached out to me. After sharing my story and offering hope for the future, the inevitable question came from the husband: "What do I do from here to get free?"

This is one of the most common questions I receive—whether I am ministering in the United States or abroad. It is a natural progression after hearing my story, which I will share in detail in Chapter 2. The question comes from people ranging from young to old, male and female, and from a variety of Christian backgrounds. It seems the destructive force of pornography spans all ages, classes and cultures. Some ask the question because of their personal struggles and others in concern for a friend or loved one in bondage. At one point in time, I was asking this question myself. For many years, I was unable to find a reliable answer. I had tried many avenues, such as books, Bible studies, psychiatry, recovery groups and counseling sessions, but the answer always seemed to elude me. I wondered if freedom from porn was even possible, and if so, why it seemed so out of reach.

After years of bondage, I concluded that I was likely destined to remain hopelessly addicted to pornography. Perhaps others had somehow broken out of its bonds, but freedom just did not seem to be in the cards for me. However, the Lord proved this conclusion to be false when He did something amazing and unexpected in my life: *He set me gloriously free from those chains that had bound me for so long.* Now—many years later—I am not only convinced that freedom is available, but that it is accessible to anyone who is willing to do it God's way.

WHO IS THIS BOOK FOR?

Many reading these words right now are all too aware of the devastating consequences of porn addiction. Maybe you have been enslaved to porn for many years, or you are just in the beginning stages of this battle. You may have already attempted to break free through other resources but to no avail. Your life might feel more like the Israelites wandering around Mount Sinai in the book of Numbers than it does the abundant life that Jesus promised in John 10. If any of these descriptions fit your current condition…and you truly desire to be free…this book is for you.

Delete is not intended to be an extensive study on pornography or the physiological effects of porn in a man's life. Some presentations on this topic are mainly educational in nature. While there is some value in understanding the biological impacts of porn, it is my conviction that an enslaved Christian man does not need more knowledge to get free. What he desperately needs is a spiritual breakthrough. This is why my goal is to provide a very practical—yet biblical—approach to this topic. This book is not a magical cure or an easy-button fix. If anyone has convinced you that either of those exist, you have been lied to. The path is difficult. It involves a spiritual battle, but one that *you are able to win with God's help!*

Over the years, I have found myself repeatedly sharing the principles of this book to men who are trapped in sexual sin. And I hope it will feel like we are sitting across the table from each other at a coffee shop, which has been a common setting for such conversations. Just like in those meetings, I want to share with any man willing to listen about how to walk in the same freedom that I have experienced since 2011.

While I understand that pornography is a growing issue among women in our day, I am writing this book specifically for men. Statistically, the issue is greater among the male population. But the main reason is that I do not feel qualified to address the unique challenges that women face in this arena. While some of the practical advice contained here could certainly be beneficial to struggling women, please understand that I will speak with a struggling Christian man in mind.

I also want to mention that I wrote this book primarily from the perspective of a married man whose battle is heterosexual in nature. Most of the examples provided will come from that vantage point. While I understand that same-sex attraction is an issue for some, and that the world of pornography is filled with homosexual content, I wrote from my personal perspective. However, all the principles included in *Delete* will apply to both single and married men who are battling with either form of lust, despite the examples provided.

My intention here is to help men who are struggling with pornography at varying degrees, from the "casual user" to the one who has spent many years in its grip. However, for those who are deeply bound in a lifestyle of sexual sin, simply reading a book and gaining some practical tools may not be enough. For a book that covers sexual sin more broadly, I would highly recommend Steve Gallagher's book, *At the Altar of Sexual Idolatry*. For those who feel they need either an at-home program or residential facility, I would refer you to Pure Life Ministries. Their contact information can be found in the back of this book.

In addition, you might know someone who is hooked on porn, and you have felt helpless to give him any advice. *Delete* can be an effective resource to help you come alongside him to provide spiritual support.*** Pastors and counselors will also find its practical nature a useful tool to help those under their care.

This book is written specifically for a Christian audience. While someone who has not turned his life over to Christ might find some value in the content, I am writing with the assumption that readers have some sort of connection with Christ. This is because I am fully convinced that true freedom from any bondage is only possible through the power of God. While someone can outwardly stop an addiction, such as drugs, alcohol, pornography or gambling without Jesus, the true heart change needed comes exclusively through His power. Just getting pornography out of a man's life has limited value if he still lacks eternal life. For this reason, the power available to overcome addiction cannot be found in a book or a process, unless it points to the cross.

While many churchgoers will assume they understand what that means, I want to make something clear at the onset of our journey. Encountering the life-transforming power of the cross is not necessarily the same as being baptized or belonging to a Christian community. It does not come from amassing head-knowledge about the Scriptures. In fact, I have met men who can very effectively communicate truths from the Bible but are very ineffective at living them out. There is a fundamental difference between knowing about Jesus and actually experiencing His power in your life. So, my assumption of each reader is that his heart is at least open to the idea of

---

***Appendix F is dedicated to helping men use *Delete* as a mentoring resource.

fully surrendering his life to Jesus in his pursuit of freedom. Refusing to do so will render most principles of this book ineffective.

PRACTICAL CONSIDERATIONS

As you progress through *Delete*, you will find three helpful tools to assist in engaging with the material on a more meaningful level:

Prayer Points

Each chapter includes prayer points that are targeted at various aspects of pornography's impact on the world around us. I encourage you to take time to pray for the needs as they are presented. While you might feel unqualified to pray for others due to your own bondage, please join me in praying for these important needs regardless of those feelings of inadequacy. In Chapter 11, we will discuss the important connection between developing a concern for the needs of others and your personal battle against porn. At this point, I would simply encourage you to practice this discipline and trust the Lord to use your prayers. He is both a prayer-hearing and prayer-answering God.

Discussion Questions

Questions designed to invoke thoughtful insight have been included after each chapter. These can be used for individual study, group discussions or counseling homework and are important to engage with as you walk through each chapter's contents. In order to get the most out of *Delete*, it is highly recommended that you take time to write out your answers in a journal. Personal Application questions are also included to help you apply the principles to your own unique situation.

Appendices

There are a variety of appendices at the back of the book that contain practical tools and resources. One challenge of writing a book like this is that technology and resources are constantly changing. While an effort was made to provide the most up-to-date resources vetted by professionals, these may change and need to be updated in future editions. In order to obtain the most up-to-date information about tools and resources, please access the web links in the back of the book.

If you are still reading these words, I assume you are the right fit for *Delete's* content. I pray that the Holy Spirit will make the truths in the following pages real to you. May the Lord bless you richly as you take steps in the direction of deleting porn from your life God's way!

Pursuing Freedom Together,

Dustin Renz

INTRO

Start:// the-journey-begins

PRAYER POINTS

- Pray about your personal journey as you begin reading *Delete*. The following are specific ways to pray:

  * Pray that the Holy Spirit will illuminate the Scriptures and principles as you encounter them along the way

  * Pray for an openness in your heart to the conviction and guidance of the Holy Spirit

  * Pray that any obstacles you are experiencing will be revealed and removed by God throughout the process

  * Pray that God will give you a desperation to get free that will lead to action

DISCUSSION QUESTIONS

1. This chapter mentions a question that many men are asking: "What do I do now to get free?" How would you answer that question based on your experience?

2. What do you think is the greatest obstacle that most men face in getting free from pornography?

3. If you had to make a guess, how many men in Christian churches do you think struggle with pornography?

4. Do you think this topic is one that is commonly talked about in Christian circles or mostly avoided? What has been your experience either way?

5. How would you respond to the following quote from the introduction:

   "I am fully convinced that true freedom from any bondage is only possible through the power of God. While someone can outwardly stop an addiction, such as drugs, alcohol, pornography or gambling without Jesus, the true heart change that we all need comes exclusively through His power."

PERSONAL APPLICATION QUESTIONS

1. What are your personal expectations as you approach this book?

2. How do you feel about the prospects of freedom? Encouraged, discouraged, hopeful, doubtful, skeptical, etc. Explain why you feel that way.

3. Consider the assumptions and biases that you personally bring to this topic. Are you willing to consider the content with an open heart or are you resistant to hearing another perspective?

PART ONE:// the-problem

Caps Lock:// the-epidemic

OUSTON, WE HAVE A PROBLEM... It has been said that this is one of the most widely repeated misquotes in American history. Most people understand the context of this famous phrase due to the influence of Hollywood. John Swigert—an astronaut aboard Apollo 13 on its third moon-landing mission—contacted the controllers in Houston to report a problem that had occurred on the spacecraft. In the award-winning film named after the space vessel, the writers decided to change the verbiage of this historic moment to increase its dramatic effect. However, the original transcript from the Apollo 13 message reveals that Swigert actually said, "Houston, we've had a problem."[1]

This small alteration in tense might seem inconsequential. But the purpose of the historical conversation was alluding to the fact that the spacecraft had a problem that had already been resolved. However, referring to a fixed problem does not make for exciting cinema. So, the phrase, "Houston, we have a problem," came into existence and most assume that this is the original quote from John Swigert.

When it comes to the epidemic of pornography in our society—especially in the church world—I wish the original quote was a more accurate description. I want to hope that one day, we can look back over the landscape of time and say, "We have had an intense battle with sexual immorality in the church, but that is a thing of the past." Yet, without the supernatural intervention of God, I fear the problem will remain present tense for some time to come…if not indefinitely. And I intend to do anything possible to change the tense of the crisis, at least for as many men as are willing to take the journey with me.

THE FACTS OF THE MATTER

We have a major epidemic on our hands. An epidemic is defined as, "a widespread occurrence of an infectious disease in a community at a particular time."[2] While I am not referring to a physical virus or transmittable disease, this is an apt description of what is taking place in a spiritual sense. If you are an active participant in the Christian community—and have any level of awareness at all—no doubt you agree. One might expect unbelievers to freely indulge in sexual sin, but what is even more alarming is the skyrocketing rate of pornography in the church. The statistics being generated suggest that more than one-half of Christian men are involved with pornography on a regular basis. One survey even states that 97% of professing Christian men have been exposed to porn![3] If that does not startle you, I do not know what will.

Take a look at these staggering statistics from several studies:

- 57% of pastors said porn addiction is the most damaging issue in their congregation[4]

- 75% of Christian men reported that they are viewing pornography at least occasionally[5]

- 55% of married Christian men said they look at pornography at least monthly and 35% had an extramarital affair[6]

- 57% of pastors and 64% of youth pastors admitted they have struggled with porn[7]

- 86% of pastors felt porn use is common among Christian pastors[8]

The existence of pornography in the church is a tragic reality. Even if these statistics were grossly exaggerated, to have even *a fragment of men* who profess Christ bound to porn is a call for alarm. Statistics from a survey seem less jarring than considering the possibility that the men sitting on each side of me on Sunday morning are likely bound in sexual sin. Pornography is the elephant in the room that no one wants to talk about. But facts like these should propel us into action. In fact, they should cause those involved with porn to fall on their knees and cry out to the Lord to set them free.

The Apostle Paul tells us plainly that sexual sin should not even be named among the Christian community in Ephesians 5:3. The NIV states, "Among you there must not be even a hint of sexual immorality." The Greek word being used for *a hint* is *onomazó*, and it means, "things which are called by their own name because they are present or exist."[9] Essentially, Paul is saying, "If you are trying to find sexual immorality in this world, the last place you should be able to find it is in the church of Jesus Christ." If the statistics above hold true in the typical church today, not only is there a hint of sexual immorality in the Christian community, but it is actually thriving among us.

The most tragic aspect of this discussion is knowing that there will be men who read these words and experience the conviction of the Holy Spirit yet will choose to harden their hearts and reject the only One who can set them free. Perhaps they will remember some of the principles in this book at a later date and eventually respond. But I know all too well that tomorrow is not promised. My own past confirms that putting off that decision only causes your heart to harden more. That is why the writer of Hebrews says, "*Today*, if you will hear His voice, do not harden your hearts."[10]

So many times, when I am sharing with a group of men, I can hear the enemy whispering in my ear: "None of these men need to hear this. Look at them. These are good Christians. You have the wrong group." If I did not know better, I might take the bait and address the topic with less fervency or even not at all. But I have had too many conversations around my book table when no one else is around, and men feel free to share their deep, dark secrets. I have too often been pulled into hallways with men who lower their voices and glance nervously over their shoulders, as if they are making a drug deal. Those conversations typically start off with the words, "I've never told anyone what I am about to tell you." My greatest fear for those men is that our short interaction will be the extent of their confession. After all, it is much easier to expose your sin to a stranger than to the people who really need to know.

PORN IS CALLING YOUR NAME

The point is that the modern church is in a mess. Sexual sin has invaded our camp and rendered many men spiritually powerless. And it is no wonder considering the role that society's technological advancements have played in escalating this issue. Think about the world in which we live today. The ease with which men can find and view pornography is astounding. You do not even have to go looking for porn; it is hunting for you. Like the devil going back and forth, roaming the earth,[11] the pornography industry is actively seeking out its next victim. What that looks like in the natural realm is a massive industry managed by corrupt and greedy people who are working tirelessly to exploit our sexual desires. Their end goal is to transfer *our* money into *their* bank accounts. But in the spiritual realm, the devil and his demons are using this industry to transfer the souls of men into hell. He is playing for keeps and, tragically, his strategy has been very effective.

Today, porn is promoted through so many channels, it is almost impossible to avoid exposure on some level unless you live in the wilderness without any connection to the outside world. One survey reported that the majority of kids are exposed to porn by age thirteen, with some exposed as young as seven[12] and that 94% of children will see porn by the age of fourteen.[13] Another found that "nearly three-quarters of young adults and half of teens come across what they consider to be porn at least once a month, whether they are seeking it or not."[14] Porn producers know that they only need to get their content in front of the average male in our culture, and they will have a steady, oftentimes lifelong customer. They bait us with a seemingly endless supply of free material. Like the drug dealer who gets their victim high for free until they get hooked, pornographers dangle carrots in front of potential customers, knowing they just need to get them to click on a link and then let curiosity do the rest of the work. We are experiencing the exploitation of sexuality in our culture at an unprecedented level.

I have met many men whose first exposure to pornography happened completely on accident as a young boy on the internet. Pornography pushers are not stupid. They spend millions on advertising to make sure that their graphic smut is as visible and accessible as possible. The invention of smartphones created a world where a man can have unlimited access to the filthy world of porn tucked away neatly in his pocket. There was a time not long ago when the only way to find porn was in an adult bookstore. This required a potential customer to be in contact with other people to pursue their lust. Often, that risk alone was enough to keep otherwise curious men from taking the plunge. To say that times have changed is a gross understatement. It is more like we are living in a different galaxy.

SOCIETY MADE ME DO IT!

Is the fact that men in our culture are under so much pressure to give in to pornography an excuse for sin? Does the constant barrage of sensuality in the Western world necessitate some involvement in perversion? Should we have the attitude, "Well, it's just the culture we live in. How can you expect anything else?" Emphatically no! A Christian is called to resist culture when its values are contrary to the clear teachings of Scripture. We are commanded in Romans 12:2 to avoid becoming conformed to the world, and certainly that would include the ungodly—and demonic—world of porn.

While our culture undoubtedly plays a key role in our struggle to live in purity, we cannot lower the standards of Scripture to let ourselves off the hook. As we will learn in Chapter 4, the Bible is not silent on this issue, even though it was written long before adult bookstores, magazines, websites and smartphones ever came into existence. We might live in a war zone, but that simply means we need to become *war*-riors. The unbiblical values of the culture in which we are surrounded should not be viewed as a neutral necessity but as an enemy to overcome.

Unfortunately, too many men in the church have already caved. They took the bait and drank the poison. They are far from rising as warriors in our generation and are instead burying their heads in the sand of passivity. They are called to be the spiritual priests of their home, but they have relegated that responsibility to their wives, who were never meant to shoulder the spiritual oversight of their families alone. These men are called to be the protectors of their wives and children. Instead, they have become a threat to them as they have opened their homes to demonic and worldly influences through the sexual sin to which they have joined themselves. They are supposed to be men of purity, honor, integrity and holiness, and yet their minds are given over to sensuality, lust, covetousness and perversion. The Christian man given over to pornography is a spiritual coward. I speak these words—not in a condemning tone—but from experience because I used to be one myself.

LURED AWAY INTO SIN

A story from the Old Testament provides a picture of what is happening to men in our churches. Recall the story of Balak the king of Moab, who hired the prophet Balaam to curse the Israelites. Despite being paid to curse God's people, Balaam blessed them instead. And he did this, not just once, but three times, much to King Balak's chagrin. Right after this event, Numbers 25 opens with this statement:

Now Israel remained in Acacia Grove, and the people began to commit harlotry [sexual immorality] with the women of Moab.

They invited the people to the sacrifices of their gods, and the people ate and bowed down to their gods. So Israel was joined to Baal of Peor, and the anger of the Lord was aroused against Israel.
(**Numbers 25:1-3**)

Due to their sin, a plague broke out and 24,000 people died. The way this passage is recorded almost seems like an isolated incident from the previous story about Balak and Balaam. However, we discover something interesting about the Moabite women in Numbers 31. Moses states:

Look, these women caused the children of Israel, through the counsel of Balaam, to trespass against the Lord in the incident of Peor, and there was a plague among the congregation of the Lord.
(**Numbers 31:16**)

In this passage, we discover that the seduction of the Israelites was actually Balaam's idea. He exploited their sexual weakness to get them to succumb to temptation. Since he was not able to pronounce a curse on them himself, he decided to tempt them into their own self-destruction. This caused them to incur the wrath of the God by their own sinful actions. The Book of Revelation echoes this thought in Jesus' message to the church in Pergamum:

You have there those who hold the doctrine of Balaam, who taught Balak to put a stumbling block before the children of Israel, to eat things sacrificed to idols, and to commit sexual immorality.
(**Revelation 2:14**)

The enemy of God's people had a specific strategy to destroy them. His plan was to introduce promiscuous women into their camp who were willing to have sex with the men under the guise of worship, causing them to turn their backs on Yahweh. These men were supposed to be warriors, passionate about the honor of the God of Israel. Instead, they folded under the pressure when it mattered most.

How similar are men in the church today? An identical strategy has been unleashed on the church through pornography. And unfortunately—just like in the Book of Numbers—it has been successful. A seductive spirit has crept into the camp. And many men have been fooled hook, line and sinker. They have been emasculated spiritually and cannot fulfill their role as godly men because of the sin in their lives. But there is hope, because one man became the hero of the story in Numbers, and his name is Phinehas.

> And indeed, one of the children of Israel came and presented to his brethren a Midianite woman in the sight of Moses and in the sight of all the congregation of the children of Israel, who were weeping at the door of the tabernacle of meeting. Now when Phinehas the son of Eleazar, the son of Aaron the priest, saw it, he rose from among the congregation and took a javelin in his hand; and he went after the man of Israel into the tent and thrust both of them through, the man of Israel, and the woman through her body. So the plague was stopped among the children of Israel. **(Numbers 25:6-8)**

In Phinehas, we find a man who was passionate for holiness and the glory of the Lord. He did what he could to put an end to the sexual immorality that was destroying the Israelite army. And I believe the Lord wants to turn all of us into men like Phinehas. He is looking for those who will not only fight for their own purity but will contend for their fellow brothers in Christ. We need to become men who are fed up with the enemy ravaging the church uncontested. If that describes you, I want to lock arms with you in combat. This is not a battle for the faint of heart, but it is my testimony as well as countless others that victory is possible. May the Lord raise up a generation of men with the zeal and boldness of Phinehas! And I pray that every man reading these words is numbered among them.

BIG PROBLEM, BIGGER SAVIOR

Yes, we have a big problem, and it is a present-tense problem. The issue of pornography in the church is large in magnitude and powerful in its ability to deceive. It is emasculating men in both the pulpit and the pew. Many church leaders are wondering what they can do to help men under their care to find freedom. At times, it can be overwhelming. The temptation might be to throw up our hands in defeat and withdraw. But these are the responses that the enemy desires.

Instead of focusing on the giant problem in our way, we need to turn our intention to the fact that we have a mountain-moving Savior. We have a more powerful cross. And we have a God who is ready and willing to tear down strongholds and confront the lies of the enemy that paralyze us. If you desire to delete pornography from your life, take heart! You have a Savior who wants you to find freedom even more than you want to obtain it.

Victory will not come to those who are looking for the path of least resistance. It is reserved for the courageous men who can say, "Whatever it takes, I want to be free." Only the ones who are truly ready to do business with God will find the breakthrough that they desire. My prayer for each man reading these words is that the day will come in the not too distant future that you can share your testimony in the past tense: "Houston, I *had* a problem…but because of what God did in my life, I'm now walking in freedom!"

Are you ready? Great! We will dive in together. First, I want to share my personal battle with pornography that began when I was very young. This was long before my battle with porn would become past tense.

CHAPTER 1

Caps Lock:// the-epidemic

PRAYER POINTS

- Pray for men in the church who profess Christ and yet are hooked on pornography

- Pray that God will give supernatural wisdom to church leaders on how to lead men into purity

- Pray that ministers who are bound in sin will have the courage to deal with it

DISCUSSION QUESTIONS

1. Based on your personal experience, what is your perspective on the statistics offered in this chapter? Do they seem realistic? Why do you feel that way?

2. Can you relate to the feeling that porn is a constant source of temptation around the typical man?

3. How has the advancement of technology played a role in encouraging a sexualized culture?

4. What are some of the excuses that men typically use to avoid taking responsibility for their purity?

5. In the story of Phinehas from Numbers 25, what character qualities did he exhibit that men in sexual sin need to develop?

PERSONAL APPLICATION QUESTIONS

1. Are you tempted to blame society or other people for your struggle with sexual sin? In what ways have you been tempted to do this?

2. What role have your personal decisions had in embracing pornography in your life?

3. Does sexual sin seem bigger and more powerful than Jesus to you right now? Write out a prayer asking God to increase your faith in His ability to set you free.

2

Enter:// my-story

I WANT TO SHARE MY PERSONAL BATTLE with porn for two reasons. First and foremost, I know that it brings glory to God. Secondly, I have seen how the Lord uses it to provide hope to men who need it. While the details of my situation will be different from yours, the spiritual battle is the same. Understanding my back story will also provide important context for the rest of the content of this book.

As a man in my forties, I have witnessed a breathtaking increase in technology over the years, as well as the depths of depravity that have come along with it. I have observed our culture sinking into the bottomless pit of unprecedented sexual immorality. However, my first exposure to pornography came even before the internet had been piped into residential homes.

I grew up on an island in southwest Florida. While my childhood memories are few and hazy, the day that I was first exposed to pornography at around seven years old, is one that I have never been able to erase from my mind. I was in elementary school and was waiting at my bus stop at a community civic center just down the road from our house. It was meant to be a safe place for the community to gather, but my otherwise innocent life was radically altered there that day.

Some of the neighborhood boys told me to climb into a large banyan tree because they had something to show me. I cannot recall if they told me in advance what was hidden there, but there was no way my childlike mind would have been able to comprehend what they were saying even if they had. I was certainly oblivious to the fact that I was walking into a situation that would open the door of my heart to almost twenty years of sexual addiction.

If I could somehow go back in time as an adult and speak to myself on that day, I suppose I would do anything I could to convince myself to stay as far away from that tree as possible. I would tell seven-year-old Dustin, "If you look at what those boys want to show you, it is going to cost you more than you could ever imagine. It is going to pervert your sexual desires and cause you to live in spiritual darkness. It will almost destroy your marriage and family one day. In fact, it will nearly cost you your soul!"

I wish I could somehow wipe away that event from the timeline of my life. But God did not create life with a Backspace key, despite the fact we have all wished at some point in our lives that He had. When the boys took me into that tree, and opened the cover of that magazine, it was like they opened a new world to me. I saw images that I have never been able to get out of my head, even decades later. It was the first time I could remember seeing adults naked, and certainly the first time that I had ever seen people involved in the depraved acts that were portrayed there.

Looking back, the events of that day did not seem as epic in nature as I am describing them now. My first exposure to porn did not plunge me into an immediate pursuit of illicit sex. Nor did I spend every waking minute wishing I could get back to that magazine. In fact, not long after that first encounter, I would be confessing to my mother in tears because I felt dirty and I knew that something was wrong. She would then locate the magazine and destroy it. But unfortunately for me—and I imagine for the others who were exposed to it—the destruction of the physical magazine could not remove the hooks that were already in my heart.

CONTINUED ACCESS

Regrettably, that was not the only time I was exposed to porn as a child. I had a childhood friend whose parents had pornographic cable channels. Later, I stumbled upon a pornographic VHS (if you can remember what those were), stuck it into the player and was once again brought into this strange world that I seemed to keep discovering accidentally. I had no concept of spiritual warfare or demonic spirits at the time, but looking back, it is obvious that there were forces outside of myself involved in all of this. I had continuous access to pornographic material at varying levels throughout my childhood.

As the years progressed, pornography ceased to be something that I was unwittingly exposed to and became something that I both desired and pursued. The process of puberty and the discovery of the habit of masturbation played a key role in the development of my sexual lust. It was like gasoline had been poured into a smoldering fire. Fantasy became a deeply ingrained habit, as I learned that I could pursue sexual pleasure in the secrecy of my thoughts.

My fascination with sexual content continued throughout middle school. This involved watching scrambled cable TV channels, sex scenes in movies and eventually taking the risk of renting a post office box and subscribing to *Playboy* magazine. That required a lot more courage, but my lust was growing stronger than my common sense could control.

Everything eventually changed as I entered high school and the internet became available. I discovered, via dial-up internet, that I had access to a world that made magazines and R-rated movies seem like child's play. Suddenly, an endless plethora of video clips were available at my fingertips, and the risk level of getting caught was minimized. For all the good that can be accomplished through internet technology, the evils that have been unleashed seem to overshadow them all. If pornography had its grip on me before that moment, it now had a choke hold on my soul.

I should mention that, although pornography is the focus of this book, the sexual sin of fantasy, masturbation and eventually fornication were all byproducts of my porn addiction. From the time I was originally exposed to porn, sexual sin was an ever-growing monster inside of me. It only escalated through the years as I grew older. Acting out what I had been watching others do became an insatiable desire.

I am ashamed to say that I treated my virginity like a red-hot coal in my lap. To me, it was something that I had to rid myself of as quickly as possible. There was a great deal of pressure in high school to have sex, and I bought into the lie that virginity was something to be despised. I was fourteen when that happened, and it led to numerous impure relationships and sexual encounters. I look at fourteen-year-olds today and I think, "You are only a child." How I could have been so deceived and hooked by sin at that age is shocking to me as an adult. All of this is a source of deep shame and regret to me now.

ENTER JESUS

By the time I was eighteen, I had left behind me a wake of devastation. My obsession with porn coupled with a raging drug and alcohol addiction, led to sexual encounters with multiple people, and nothing seemed to quench the lust in my soul. Each experience only caused me to crave greater levels of degradation. None of it provided lasting satisfaction but just enough excitement and pleasure to leave me crying out for more. I shudder to think of where that path may have led me had I not found myself in a Christian drug and alcohol program called Teen Challenge where I encountered Christ.

I want to be clear that I did not enter Teen Challenge hoping for any kind of spiritual breakthrough. In fact, I had determined in my heart that I would not allow the program to brainwash me with religion. My sole reason for entering the program was to sober up enough to get my addiction under control and be able to go back to my lifestyle of sex and drugs without hitting rock bottom again. However, I found myself in an environment with other men with similar backgrounds whose lives were being transformed. And they told me it was Jesus who was changing them.

My skepticism and general distaste for Christianity slowly eroded, but not without a battle. I fought against the Holy Spirit's invitation into a new life in Christ. One day, after a significant spiritual battle, I decided to do what I was told by the leadership of the program. I got on my hands and knees and asked God to get me out of the tangled mess of my life. That prayer of surrender set my life on a completely new—and unexpected—trajectory.

My conversion experience was anything but dull. When I came to faith in Jesus, everything changed, and I had a newfound desire for holiness in my life. It was not just a decision I made to try to be a better person, it was a radical transformation out of darkness and into His wonderful light.[1] I became a new creation, with the old things passing away.[2] I fell in love with Jesus, longed to spend time in prayer and worship, and felt called into the ministry, something no one would have expected. I had a sincere desire to please God and I was grateful for the amazing work that He had done in my life. It seemed that the future was bright for me.

By the time I graduated the program and began working in the office as an administrator, I had been free from porn and masturbation for nearly a year. However, being placed in an environment with an internet connection and no accountability proved to be too great a temptation for me. I began to dabble. It was not something I immediately plunged into. It started with looking at swimsuit pics. I remember feeling so convicted and even reaching out to someone for prayer. But, little by little, the search terms became increasingly degraded, and soon pornography took hold of my heart once again.

THE WORST DECISION I COULD HAVE MADE

I enrolled in Bible school to train for ministry while still working part-time at Teen Challenge on the weekends. I had a sincere desire to serve the God who had rescued me out of a lifestyle of sin, crime and addiction. It was at that school that I met my wife, Brittany, during my first semester. I had no interest in dating at the time, but she came into my life unexpectedly and we fell in love. I was fully convinced then (and still now) that she was the woman that the Lord wanted me to marry. As we were getting more serious, I confessed everything about my sin to her. I will never forget the heaviness of that moment. She had saved her virginity for marriage and prayed for a Christian husband who had done the same. Then I came along with all the baggage of my past and even active sin in my life. It did not seem like a fair trade.

Brittany rightfully insisted that I completely rid my life of the porn or discontinue the relationship. I attempted to get counseling at the school, but when freedom did not come after a few sessions, I did what I had learned to do throughout my pre-Christian years: I began to lie and pretend nothing was going on. Unfortunately, I had already mastered the art of manipulation and covering up sin incredibly well. Those skills would prove to be my greatest enemy in the years to come.

A few days before we got married, I looked at pornography for what I claimed would be the last time. I expected that marriage was going to make the problem go away. However, the pornography that I kept hidden in the dark followed me down the aisle like an annoying dog nipping at my heels. I could not seem to shake it even after entering married life. In some ways, I truly desired to be free. It was not that I was shamelessly viewing pornography on a regular basis with no sense of guilt. I always felt terrible about it. The conviction of the Holy Spirit kept me from any sense of satisfaction that I should have found in Christ. It was not that I made no effort to stop. I wanted to live a pure life, but I never seemed to be able to. I always told myself that I could privately handle it with God. That kind of thinking kept me in sin for years. I was miserable living a secret life and always vowed it would be the last time. But that "last time" never came, and I began to despair that I would ever find freedom.

The lies continued and I became bolder as time went on. Shortly after our wedding, I applied to enter the ministry through our denomination. Walking through that process forced me into situations that either demanded I come clean about my sin or dig myself in a deeper hole with more deception. Tragically, I chose the latter and was given a license to preach under false pretenses of a holy life.

My shameful testimony was that I lied to stay married. I lied to stay in ministry. I lied to get on the mission field. And despite my mistaken belief that moving to the other side of the world would help me overcome my problem, I found that my pornography obsession bought a plane ticket on the same flight to Eastern Europe. After a year and a half on the mission field, I finally stopped lying.

EVERYTHING FALLS APART...BUT GOD

My secret life came to light in a completely unexpected way. One morning, Brittany asked me, "What is going on with you?" Although I had no previous intention of exposing my secrets, I told her everything. It was as if the Lord had had enough of the lies and was not going to allow me to do work for His kingdom with so much hidden darkness. That confession caused what felt like a massive explosion in our lives. My wife had to come to grips with the fact that the man she had been married to for six years was in many ways a total stranger. Our missionary career came to an abrupt halt, and we were flown back to the United States three days later and asked to resign. My preaching credentials were suspended, and we ended up living in my in-law's basement in Ohio with our two-month-old daughter. It was as if my confession upended every part of our lives. Unfortunately for my family, the devastation from my sin would continue for the next eight months.

I spent those months outwardly doing what I was asked to do, including seeing a Christian psychologist, taking psychotropic medication, meeting with a pastor and living under strict rules regarding my use of time and money. However, none of these external factors could reach a heart that was still desperate for drugs and porn. At one point, my wife finally had enough of the lies and manipulation and gave me an ultimatum: either I enter a residential program called Pure Life Ministries in Dry Ridge, Kentucky or find somewhere else to live.

Somehow the Lord was able to get me to Pure Life, although I went very reluctantly. I will be eternally grateful that He did because it was in that place that I had an encounter with the Lord which literally saved my soul. It was there that my freedom from many years of pornography and drug addiction began.

The remainder of this book will draw from the foundational truths and experiences I received from the Lord during my time at Pure Life

Ministries. What God has done in my marriage, family, ministry and relationship with Him could fill a book of its own. I am continuously in awe of His work in my life. His mercy has proven itself infinitely more powerful than any temptation or lust of the flesh. He has done what I never believed was possible.

If nothing else, my prayer is that reading my story will provide you with hope for your own life and cause you to think, "If God can set that guy free, maybe He can set me free too." But even if my story sounds lightweight in comparison to the level of addiction you are trapped in, there is still hope for *you!*

Maybe you have tried everything you could think of, to no avail. Perhaps you have already read books, online articles, attended conferences and prayed every prayer you know to pray. Maybe you have seen counselors and tried to work through this issue before. None of that intimidates me, because I know what the Lord has done, not only in my life, but in the lives of so many others.

As previously mentioned, I do not intend to provide a simple formula to freedom because I do not believe there is one. But there is a cross. There is repentance. And there is a God who will fight on your behalf in this battle against hell. But you must take the first step.

We will continue in the next chapter by providing a scriptural basis for God's design for sex.

CHAPTER 2

Enter:// my-story

PRAYER POINTS

- Pray that God will give you a fresh revelation of the cross of Calvary

- Pray that anyone in your life you know who is in bondage to sexual sin will find true and lasting freedom through Christ

- Pray that anyone you know personally who is not born again will encounter Jesus and be saved

DISCUSSION QUESTIONS

1. What is it about the nature of sexual sin that makes it so easy for a man to get entangled in its web?

2. Do you believe that Jesus has the power to set a man completely free from porn? Why or why not?

3. What are some of the main reasons a professing Christian would be tempted to hide his sin from others?

4. How have you seen society evolving from your childhood until today? In what ways have those changes contributed to the problem of sexual immorality?

5. What do you think are the greatest obstacles that men today face to maintain sexual purity?

PERSONAL APPLICATION QUESTIONS

1. Without going into unnecessary detail, take a moment to share how pornography has impacted your personal life, family, friends and community.

2. How have you seen the Lord reaching out to you in your life and drawing you to Him? What specific examples can you provide of God's attempt to intervene in your situation?

3. What evidence can you see of the devil's hand in your life to keep you from experiencing freedom and growing closer to the Lord?

3

Function:// reclaiming-sex

HAVE YOU EVER BEEN TEMPTED TO blame God for your porn problem because He gave you a sex drive? From our human perspective, it can almost seem like a cruel joke. God created men with a sex drive that is fueled by hormones. He designed a system that periodically causes pressure both emotionally and physically. He made men visual creatures, stimulated by the things we see. Then, He filled the world with beautiful creatures that captivate our attention and arouse our desires. It seems like we have been set up for failure. The temptation is to think something like this: "God, if you hadn't given me this sex drive, I wouldn't have any problems. I wish you would just take this desire away. My life would be so much easier!"

While this sentiment might be common among Christian males, it is important to understand that our drive for sex is a gift from God. It is not His fault that we have allowed it to become something He never intended it to be. So many men ask the Lord to take away their sexual desires because they want an easy fix. But the solution is not to somehow overthrow our sex drive. What we need to do is to create a biblical view of sex and a healthy way to manage the desires within us. The male sex drive is not the problem. Rather, our struggle comes from the unhealthy way we manage it.

The Bible clearly teaches that God is the Creator of everything, and therefore, He determines how the world is supposed to function. It is only the Lord who can decide what is good and what is evil. It is important to affirm these truths because we live in an age when the culture around us is challenging them, calling them outdated, irrelevant and out of touch with modern reality. Even the most basic biological realities are being challenged, such as the belief that there are only two genders which are assigned at conception. So, it is vital that we revisit the original design for human sexuality.

Let us begin where the Bible describes the creation of humanity:

So God created man in His own image; in the image of God He created him; male and female He created them. Then God blessed them, and God said to them, "Be fruitful and multiply; fill the earth and subdue it; have dominion over the fish of the sea, over the birds of the air, and over every living thing that moves on the earth." (Genesis 1:27-28)

Here, the Scriptures provide the creation narrative of the first two humans. These verses also include the first command given to the human race: "Be fruitful and multiply; fill the earth and subdue it..." The Creator's first recorded words to His creation were, "I want you to have sex, produce babies and multiply yourselves." Sexual intercourse was given as a gift from God, encouraged by Him, and would result in offspring who would also take part in procreation. This was all put into place by design. When God crafted the human body, all of this was taken into account.

In Genesis 2, we are told about how and why God created the

first woman. He declared that it was not good for man to be alone. (vs. 18) He then formed all the animals and brought them to Adam so that he could provide each with a name. Verse 20 states what would have been obvious to Adam throughout this process: "But for Adam there was not found a helper comparable to him." Then the creation story of the first woman is provided:

> And the Lord God caused a deep sleep to fall on Adam, and he slept; and He took one of his ribs, and closed up the flesh in its place. Then the rib which the Lord God had taken from man He made into a woman, and He brought her to the man. And Adam said: "This is now bone of my bones and flesh of my flesh; She shall be called Woman, because she was taken out of Man." Therefore a man shall leave his father and mother and be joined to his wife, and they shall become one flesh. And they were both naked, the man and his wife, and were not ashamed. **(Genesis 2:21-25)**

In these verses, we discover the first description of God's conception of marriage. It was meant to be experienced between one man and one woman in the context of a covenant relationship. The Lord meant for them to enjoy each other sexually without hindrance or shame, describing the deep intimacy that the marriage bond would create.

Jesus would later refer to this passage when He was reiterating God's intention for marriage in a discussion with the Pharisees:

> "But from the beginning of the creation, God 'made them male and female.' 'For this reason a man shall leave his father and mother and be joined to his wife, and the two shall become one flesh'; so then they are no longer two, but one flesh. Therefore what God has joined together, let not man separate." **(Mark 10:6-9)**

In a conversation about marriage, Jesus pointed back to this passage from Genesis to reinforce God's intention for sexuality. It provides God's original construct for sexual relationships, and we have no biblical reasoning to think that He has changed His mind. Men and women were intentionally created differently, both internally and externally, with the intention of bringing them together to become one in marriage.

Sex has always been God's idea. He is not ashamed or embarrassed by it. In fact, if you think about how the human sex drive is designed, it reveals His intricate creativity. Our reproductive organs are both complex and fascinating aspects of human anatomy. For instance, one incredible feature of sexual intercourse is that it has the ability to produce other humans, with their own body, mind, personality and DNA. What an amazing, imaginative Creator!

However, God did not just design sex to produce humans; He intentionally made it pleasurable. He designed the experience of orgasm to be one of the most physically exhilarating experiences that a man and woman can enjoy in this life. He made sex both pleasing and incredibly intimate. It is so intimate, in fact, that the Bible tells us that through the act of sexual intimacy, two people become one flesh. That is more than just a poetic way of expressing love; it is a spiritual bonding of two souls together. As C.S. Lewis once wrote:

> "The Christian idea of marriage is based on Christ's words that a man and wife are to be regarded as a single organism—for that is what the words 'one flesh' would be in modern English. And the Christians believe that when He said this He was not expressing a sentiment but stating a fact—just as one is stating a fact when one says that a lock and its key are one mechanism, or that a violin and a bow are one musical instrument."[1]

Paul also referenced the concept of oneness in 1 Corinthians 6:16. He explained, "Or do you not know that he who is joined to a harlot is one body with her? For 'the two,' He says, 'shall become one flesh.'" This is one reason why virginity is so precious and why sexual sin with another person is so grievous. Through the act of sex, we are spiritually joining ourselves to another, even if it is only a one-time encounter. We experience something with that person that is meant only for marriage, and it forms a bond we cannot simply ignore. The Bible adamantly disagrees with society's message that sex is only a physical experience and nothing more.

Sex is both good and holy when kept within God's boundaries. Hebrews 13:4 says, "Marriage is honorable among all, and the bed undefiled..." Sometimes, in Christian circles, we shy away from talking about sex due to its intimate nature. However, God's Word does not blush when it comes to physical intimacy. He designed sex, encourages sex and blesses sex...when it is experienced within His parameters.

MAN'S REFUSAL TO ENJOY SEX GOD'S WAY

Any form of sexual experience that takes place outside of a loving marriage between a husband and a wife is a perversion of God's design. History is replete with examples of how humans have refused to keep sex within His explicit boundaries. This should come as no surprise, because the first two humans were not even able to restrain themselves from eating a piece of forbidden fruit. God provided Adam and Eve clear boundaries, commanded them to avoid taking a specific action, and they went against His will and did it anyways. And every other sin that has been committed since the Garden of Eden—whether of a sexual nature or not— follows a similar pattern.

Because of that original sin, the motivation of humans has shifted from living for God's glory to living independently for self. The ensuing selfishness that came as a result affected mankind's relationship with sex, often making it something God never intended it to become. The Lord created sex for mutual pleasure and an expression of love between a husband and wife. But the sinful nature is not concerned with giving, only receiving. So, the desire to experience pleasure naturally led people to pursue sex illicitly, resulting in an abuse of God's gift.

In modern church culture, many prefer to use softer terms to describe sin, like "bad habits," "weaknesses," "hang-ups" or "struggles." We talk about "shacking up" instead of fornication and "an affair" instead of adultery. Even using the term "addiction," although an accurate assessment of those who are in bondage to pornography, is a more clinical term. We need to call it what God calls it: *sin*. There is a beauty in calling out sin for what it is because the Bible is clear that there is an antidote for it and an escape route out of its bondage through the process of repentance. This is why Jesus gave Himself as a sacrifice for our sins on the cross. When we redefine sin as nothing more than a bad habit or weakness, it loses the weight that Scripture intentionally places on it.

Through sex, the Lord has created something beautiful and deeply desirable to the human experience. However, in order to keep us within His design, He has given us boundaries. Just like the Department of Transportation installs guardrails alongside a highway to keep people from veering off the edge of a deadly cliff, the Lord has set up guardrails for our sexuality. People accurately assume that boundaries are restrictive, but the Lord gives us these restrictions *for our benefit*. He is not trying to make our lives miserable or keep us from something good: quite the contrary. The Lord is trying to prevent us from falling off a moral cliff into destruction. Some picture God as an overbearing parent, making arbitrary rules for the purpose of exerting His authority over us. That could not be further from the truth about His character. As a loving Father, He wants what is *best* for us, and He has clearly defined those boundaries in His Word.

PORNOGRAPHY DESTROYS SEX

According to Scripture, sexual pleasure enjoyed in a marital relationship is a blessing provided by God. Within that special bond, sex is meant to promote deep relational intimacy, unlike any other human experience. It is a vulnerable act, intended to open the hearts of a husband and wife to each other in a way they never share with others outside the marriage. Sex is designed to promote love and affection between spouses that enhances every other area of their marital relationship. To put it simply, sex is meant to be much more than a physical, selfish, pleasure-driven experience.

How differently pornographers depict sex! They have built an enormous money-making industry out of turning human sexuality into something base and carnal. Unbelievably, there are Christian couples who actually believe that porn can promote or enhance their sex lives. This is a convenient lie to cling to for those who want to justify their sin. The thinking is that porn can be useful to provide "inspiration" on sexual acts they can partake in. Others justify using it by saying that it is a safe way for a man to take care of his sexual appetites without acting out with others. One research study revealed that 55% of Christians "agree a person can regularly engage with pornography and still have a sexually healthy life."[2] It also reported that 48% "said they believe watching pornography can improve users' sex lives."[3] It appears that the industry's marketing tactics have been effective even in the lives of professing Christians.

This positive slant on porn could not be further from the truth. What pornographic materials actually promote is the *destruction* of sex as God intends it. In fact, pornography is one of the most damaging forces against a healthy sex life. Dr. Carol Tanksley explains:

"Pornography, like any addiction, lessens your ability to be stimulated by and enjoy the real thing. Those images stay in your head a long time. Pornography is all about sexual stimulation without having to do the work of intimacy. It skews a person's brain about what sex was intended to be, what men want, and what women want."[4]

The idea that porn fosters intimacy is a fallacy. As one married couple recently confessed to me: "Pornography has completely destroyed the intimacy in our sexual relationship."

One of the consequences of living a life given over to porn is that it changes the way a man views the act of sex. Even after getting free from its grip, this is something that needs to be addressed if he wants to enjoy a healthy sex life to its fullest potential. Pornography is an illusion. In a pure sexual experience between a husband and a wife, there are no camera men in the bedroom. There is no script to get right. There are no microphones being held up. The husband is not a paid actor, chosen for his masculine build and the wife is not a paid actress who was hired for her "perfectly shaped" body. Neither of them is being paid to portray that they are participating in the most pleasurable sexual experience possible. Yet that describes the illusion of sex that pornography promotes.

As a man meditates on that contrived sexual experience, it will twist and contort his understanding and expectation of sex. Fight the New Drug reports:

> "[Porn] can become incredibly problematic in sexual relationships, given that porn can warp expectations about sex, bodies, and relationships. In fact, one survey found that 53% of boys and 39% of girls reported believing that pornography was a realistic depiction of sex, and 44% of boys who consumed porn reported that it gave them ideas about the type of sex they wanted to try. That's especially concerning, considering that porn is wildly unrealistic and often promotes toxic tropes, including rape, incest, sexual violence, sexism, racism, etc."[5]

The first time a man is exposed to sexual content often sets the tone for his perspective on sex. From that point on, his initial experience will tend to dictate what he considers "normal." Having been exposed long before I ever had a sex education class or a talk from a parent—I experienced how pornography can completely distort a person's mind until their concept of sex is rooted in an entirely different realm from its intended design.

This type of distorted thinking is very difficult to overcome. It is only by learning about God's design for sex and continually training one's mind to reject all other perspectives, that a man can eventually delete those original concepts. It is only then that he can begin to embrace the sexual life that the Lord has deemed lawful and good. While I do not want to make it seem that it is impossible for a man's mind to be completely renewed, I also do not want to minimize pornography's negative impact on a man's perspective when he views porn.

I am so grateful that the Lord can help us renew our minds as we meditate, read and study His Word. It is in that place of continually feeding themselves with truth that men are able to take on the mind of Christ and live their lives according to His design. This is the only way to reclaim the true intention of sex in our lives. Men who have allowed the philosophies of porn to shape their perspective on sex must retrain their minds to view it from a godly perspective.

In the next chapter, we will discuss several biblical warnings about the consequences of refusing to keep our sexuality within the boundaries that God has set up for our protection.

CHAPTER 3

Function:// reclaiming-sex

PRAYER POINTS

- Pray that leaders in the Western church will have the courage and anointing to present a healthy view of sex to its congregants as well as the world around it

- Pray that our culture a will embrace a biblical view of sexuality once again

- Pray for people you know who are living outside of God's boundaries for their sexuality. Ask the Lord to reveal Himself to them and grant them repentance

DISCUSSION QUESTIONS

1. From your perspective, is the church more concerned about promoting God's design for sex or calling out sexual sin? What causes you to be convinced one way or the other?

2. Do you think that the way a church teaches (or fails to teach) about sexuality can contribute to the perspective that sex is shameful or dirty?

3. How have the loose moral principles of the world influenced the church in your opinion?

4. How do you grapple with the counter-biblical perspective that sex outside of marriage is not wrong?

5. What are the implications of the concept described in Genesis 2:24 of becoming "one flesh"? What does that mean on a physical, emotional, spiritual and psychological level for a couple regardless of their marital status?

PERSONAL APPLICATION QUESTIONS

1. How have your life experiences skewed your perspective on sex away from the biblical model revealed in this chapter?

2. Have you seen the way that pornography has "destroyed sex" in your own life as well as in society around us?

3. How much time do you take on a regular basis to read, study and meditate on the Word of God in order to have your mind renewed?

4

Refresh:// defining-sin

ONE QUALITY I APPRECIATE ABOUT THE BIBLE is how candidly it addresses common issues that people experience. Every temptation that men face can be found within its pages. God did not want us to be in the dark about sin and its consequences, and this is especially true about sexuality.

I find it noteworthy that out of the Ten Commandments that Yahweh gave to Israel, two of them directly confront sexual sin. The seventh commandment, "You shall not commit adultery," prohibits having sexual relations with a married person. The tenth commandment forbids coveting a neighbor's wife.[1] When the Lord listed the top ten moral commands for His people, twenty percent of them directly referenced sexual sin. From cover to cover, the Bible not only provides morally instructive commands about healthy and unhealthy sexuality but also included are many stories to illustrate the blessings and consequences of both. Why? He did this because He understands the human tendency to be tempted sexually and because sexual sin is a big deal.

You might wonder why this chapter needs to be included in a book like this. After all, if most men reading these words are professing Christians, would they not already understand that pornography is sinful? Well, in a survey by the Barna Group[2], the following disturbing trends in the church were identified:

- 49% said they were comfortable with the amount of pornography they consume.

- 22% felt neutral about the impact of porn, saying it is neither good nor bad for society.

- 21% of practicing Christians responded, "I wish I didn't use it as much as I do, but some is OK."

- Only 21% expressed a desire to eliminate pornography from their lives altogether.

It seems clear that the perspective of the modern church is shifting toward a more permissive stance regarding porn. Perhaps this is due to its acceptance within the larger cultural context. Or maybe it comes from a sense of defeat because it seems to be so widespread within the church. One commentator makes the following observation regarding the percentage of pastors who are in bondage to porn themselves:

"We know that pastors and leaders are shepherds...Their responsibility is to guide their sheep through the different pastures of life, and somewhere in those pastures, there's a big area called 'sexual integrity.' And a lot of shepherds are not able to lead their sheep there, because they do not have access [to it]."[3]

I suppose all of these are contributing factors to the increase in porn's tolerance in the church. When you couple that with the desire to rationalize a besetting sin, it encourages a passive stance toward it.

With those statistics in mind, I want to share five strong warnings from the New Testament about sexual immorality that should cause every believer to be greatly concerned about having any connection with porn. The Greek word used in the following verses comes from the root word *porneia*, which is where we derive the term *pornography*. It is defined as, "a selling off (surrendering) of sexual purity; promiscuity of any type."[4] Translators use different English terms for this word such as *sexual immorality* and *fornication*. So, although the Bible is not specifically referencing what you and I might think when we hear the term *pornography*, by nature, it would be included in the concept of sexual sin in the following passages.

WARNING 1:

Sexual Purity was an Expectation in the Early Church

In the book of Acts, a debate arose within the early church about the relationship between the Old Testament Law and the Gentiles who were getting saved. There were those on one side who believed the Gentiles must be circumcised and obey the Law, just like the Jews had been doing for centuries. There were others who believed that the Gentiles should not be held to those standards because of Jesus' fulfillment of the Law. This was a very controversial topic for the Jewish believers in the first century and the debate reached the Apostle James and the early church leaders in Jerusalem. A meeting was held and a letter drafted for the Gentile believers containing the final decision of the early church leadership. A portion of that letter reads:

> Therefore I judge that we should not trouble those from among the Gentiles who are turning to God, but that we write to them to abstain from things polluted by idols, from sexual immorality (*porneias*), from things strangled, and from blood.
> (Acts 15:19-20)

This passage of Scripture is very revealing about the critical importance of purity in the eyes of the early church leaders. After much prayer and deliberation, James and the other leaders of the Christian movement made the decision to boil down their instructions to the Gentiles into just three central commands. Two of them had to do with abstaining from certain foods, and the other was to avoid sexual immorality. Out of everything that the leadership could have communicated to the Gentile believers, they felt that abstinence from sexual immorality was foundational to their walk as Christians. This displays the weight that the early church leadership placed on sexual purity for believers. They certainly did not have a lackadaisical attitude toward sexual sin.

WARNING 2:

Active Sexual Sin
Led to Church Discipline

Paul had to deal with a situation in the Corinthian church involving sexual sin in their community. In 1 Corinthians 5:1, he explained, "It is actually reported that there is sexual immorality among you, and such sexual immorality that is not even named among the Gentiles—that a man has his father's wife!" Within that context, Paul wrote the following clarification:

I wrote to you in my epistle not to keep company with sexually immoral people (*pornois*). Yet I certainly did not mean with the sexually immoral people (*pornois*) of this world, or with the covetous, or extortioners, or idolaters, since then you would need to go out of the world. But now I have written to you not to keep company with anyone named a brother, who is sexually immoral (*pornos*), or covetous, or an idolater, or a reviler, or a drunkard, or an extortioner—not even to eat with such a person. (1 Corinthians 5:9-11)

This type of treatment might seem shocking and even unloving in our modern context because Western culture has perpetuated the belief that it is wrong to confront the lifestyle choices of others. Many modern pastors do not practice biblical discipline with their congregations because that secular thinking has crept into church culture. Other churches might have discipline as a policy, but do not practically implement it for fear of offending people or being seen as a church that demands too much of its members. However, this is not the intention of church discipline in the New Testament. In fact, discipline was seen as a way of helping those who were caught in the bondage of sin.

Jesus tells us in Matthew 18:15 that confronting a brother can lead to repentance. Paul tells the Corinthians that the purpose of expelling the immoral man from church fellowship was so that he could be delivered "to Satan for the destruction of the flesh, that his spirit may be saved in the day of the Lord Jesus."[5] While many of us in modern churches shudder to think of doing something like this, the expulsion of a professing Christian in active sin was meant to be an act of mercy.

In this passage, we discover Paul's conviction that the church should deal severely with people in unrepentant sexual sin, even to the point of removing them from fellowship. He did not say, "Just give them a lot of grace. We all sin so it's not really that big of a deal. It's to be expected in a world like ours." Instead, his drastic disciplinary measures only underscore how fearful he was for the unrepentant man's soul. Obviously, Paul is referring here to someone who is living in blatant sin and would certainly show grace to someone who was actively trying to get free. But his advice to the believers in Corinth about how to deal with a Christian in sexual sin is a far cry from the lack of response in the average Western church.

WARNING 3:

Sexual Sin is an Act of the Flesh

The concept of the *flesh* or the *sinful nature* is a key theme in many of Paul's epistles. The Greek word used is *sarks* and refers to the internal self-life of a person. The self-life exists to please, promote and protect self at all costs. Every man is born with it and his flesh will continue to desire sinful pleasures even after salvation. This is why the Bible instructs us to put it to death.[6] Paul provides examples of the type of actions we would expect from this unredeemed sinful nature. To the Galatian church, he wrote:

> Now the works of the flesh (*sarkos*) are evident, which are: adultery, fornication (*porneia*), uncleanness, lewdness, idolatry, sorcery, hatred, contentions, jealousies, outbursts of wrath, selfish ambitions, dissensions, heresies, envy, murders, drunkenness, revelries, and the like... **(Galatians 5:19-21)**

This list—written to contrast the fruit of the Holy Spirit—is Paul's way of providing guidelines to the church about how to identify behaviors that come from the flesh. At the top of his list is fornication (sexual immorality) and uncleanness. The Greek word for *uncleanness* is *akatharsia* and means in a moral sense, "the impurity of lustful, luxurious, profligate living."[7] Paul reminded the Galatians that he had previously warned them about these things. It seems that he found it necessary to keep this message in front of the churches of his day.

In a similar passage in Colossians, Paul talked about putting to death specific sins that "belong to our earthly nature."[8] He named the following acts of the flesh:

> ...fornication (*porneian*), uncleanness (*akatharsian*), passion (*pathos*), evil desire, and covetousness, which is idolatry. Because of these things the wrath of God is coming upon the sons of disobedience... **(Colossians 3:5-6)**

All six of these sins are affiliated with sexual immorality. The first three (fornication, uncleanness and passion) are directly connected to sexuality. *Passion*, or the word *pathos*, is defined as "raw, strong emotions which are not guided by God (like consuming lust)."[9] However, the last three (evil desires, covetousness and idolatry) are root issues that underlie the motives of a sexual sinner. Paul instructs believers to put these types of behavior (both the outward expression as well as the inward lust) to death.

Because of Paul's strong convictions about sexual sin, he warns the Corinthian church, "Flee from sexual immorality."[10] From his perspective, something that is such a clear stumbling block to the spiritual life of a Christian is nothing to toy around with. That word *flee* is from the root word *pheugó*, which means "to shun or avoid by flight."[11] It brings to mind the story of Joseph from the book of Genesis, who literally ran away from Potiphar's seductive wife when temptation came his way.[12] This is the attitude that the man of God is supposed to develop regarding sexual temptation. Scripture clearly instructs all believers to put the works of the flesh to death, including sexual sin.

WARNING 4:

Sexual Sin is a Kingdom Disqualifier

Any time the Scriptures repeat themselves, we can be sure that it is by the intentional design of the Holy Spirit, not by accident. We find this kind of pattern throughout Paul's epistles regarding sexual immorality and the Christian life. To the Corinthian church, he wrote:

Do you not know that the unrighteous will not inherit the kingdom of God? Do not be deceived. Neither fornicators (*pornoi*), nor idolaters, nor adulterers, nor homosexuals, nor sodomites, nor thieves, nor covetous, nor drunkards, nor revilers, nor extortioners will inherit the kingdom of God. **(1 Corinthians 6:9-10)**

Here, Paul is making a strong, clear statement about sexual sin, stating that it disqualifies those mentioned from inheritance in the Kingdom of God. He encouraged the Corinthian believers, "Do not be deceived." The word for *deception* here means to "go astray, get off-course; to deviate from the correct path or roam into error."[13] He warns us that we can be deceived into believing we can live in sexual immorality and still partake in God's Kingdom. He echoes this thought in his letter to the Ephesians:

But fornication (*porneia*) and all uncleanness or covetousness, let it not even be named among you, as is fitting for saints…For this you know, that no fornicator (*pornos*), unclean person, nor covetous man, who is an idolater, has any inheritance in the kingdom of Christ and God. (**Ephesians 5:3, 5**)

Once again, Paul reminds the church that sexually immoral people will have no inheritance in God's Kingdom. In fact, he promotes a *zero-tolerance policy* for sexual sin in the church. He says these sins should not even exist among the Body of Christ. This issue was so important to Paul that he made a similar statement a third time in Galatians 5:

Now the works of the flesh are evident, which are: adultery (*porneia*), fornication (*porneia*), uncleanness, lewdness…of which I tell you beforehand, just as I also told you in time past, that those who practice such things will not inherit the kingdom of God. (**vss. 19, 21**)

It seems that the Apostle was unyielding about the fact that God's New Covenant people must embrace a lifestyle of sexual purity. The implications of these passages are meant to be alarming and unwavering. Paul is calling sin by its name and explaining the eternal consequences of living in it. But what is more shocking is how many men in the modern church do not actually believe what he says. The way you know that—aside from teachers who distort the obvious implications of these passages—is that many men in the church continue to live in sexual immorality while still professing to be living for Christ.

Paul's perspective on the issue of sexual sin in the life of a believer is undisputable. It can be difficult to accept in light of how many professing Christians live in sexual sin because it calls into question their salvation. We cannot escape the fact that sexual immorality is sinful, and anyone who believes they can live in it and still have inheritance in the Kingdom of God is deceived. That point alone should cause us all to search our hearts and cry out to the Lord for a greater degree of sexual purity.

WARNING 5:

Sexual Sin Invokes the Wrath of God

Paul tells the church in Colossae that because of sexual immorality, "the wrath of God is coming upon the sons of disobedience"[14] This connection between sexual sin and God's judgment can be seen in other areas of the New Testament as well:

- "The Lord will punish all those who commit such sins [including sexual immorality], as we told you and warned you before." **(1 Thessalonians 4:6 NIV)**

- "...fornicators (*pornous*) and adulterers God will judge..." **(Hebrews 13:4)**

- "But the...sexually immoral (*pornois*)...shall have their part in the lake which burns with fire and brimstone, which is the second death." **(Revelation 21:8)**

According to these passages, the penalty for living in sexual immorality is eternal judgment. Through these verses, the Bible is extending mercy to anyone who will heed its warning. With these consequences in mind, how could our response be anything but to *seriously* and *thoroughly* inspect our lives for sexual compromise and repent where needed? My warning to any man who thinks that he can twist Scripture to accommodate porn is this: I am certain that there are far more passages that show that sexual immorality will prevent a man from entering the Kingdom of God than verses which seem to comfort those holding onto their sin. Of course, you can always find preachers and teachers who are complicit with your desire to minimize the truths of these passages and make sin seem excusable, but listening to them is a gamble that could cost you your soul.

Paul summarizes his perspective on sexual sin in his first letter to the Thessalonians:

For this is the will of God, your sanctification: that you should abstain from sexual immorality (*porneias*); that each of you should know how to possess his own vessel in sanctification and honor, not in passion of lust, like the Gentiles who do not know God...For God did not call us to uncleanness (*akatharsia*), but in holiness. Therefore he who rejects this does not reject man, but God, who has also given us His Holy Spirit. (**1 Thessalonians 4:3-5, 6-8**)

This passage reveals a sobering reality: Anyone who refuses to listen to Scripture's call to abstain from sexual sin is rejecting God Himself. That is a warning that all of us would do well to heed.

LAYING DOWN ALL OUR EXCUSES

At the risk of becoming redundant, I shared a selection of New Testament passages in order to reveal how often and how plainly the Scriptures address the topic of sexual sin. I used to live with the false belief that somehow these Scriptures did not apply to me, even though I was regularly indulging in pornography while professing Christ. I dismissed the clear warnings of Scripture and told myself that I was the "exception to the rule." After all, I knew I had been born again, and I had even been used by God in ministry. Surely, the "little" sin in my life was nothing that the Lord was too concerned about. I failed to realize what Jeremiah said about how our hearts are deceitful "above all things."[15] Is it not true that we are masters at trying to justify our actions? We tend to always believe the best about ourselves. When we are not living that out, we find ways to dismiss ourselves from responsibility. But the Scriptures are clear that sexual immorality will not go unpunished.

Just based on the fact that you chose to read this book, one could assume that you already have some conviction that pornography is sinful. However, the importance of developing true convictions about the sinfulness of pornography needs to be emphasized. If we have any gray areas in our belief system, it will be very difficult to find true freedom because there will always be a voice telling us, "It's not that big of a deal. Why are you trying so hard to fight this?"

This is the reason that we need to clearly define pornography as sin. Forgivable? Yes. Excusable? Not at all. If we keep any justifications or rationalizations intact, we give the devil and our flesh a platform for temptation that will be nearly impossible to resist. We need to reject thought patterns such as:

"God understands, I'm just a man and we are sexual creatures..."

"If my wife is okay with it, then there is nothing wrong with porn..."

"I was exposed at a young age. It's not my fault that I have this problem..."

"Everybody is doing it. It's just the society we live in..."

"It's not hurting anyone else..."

These types of statements will only serve as roadblocks to freedom. Whenever we allow flexibility in our convictions, the devil will use that to lure us back into sin. This is why it is crucial that we comprehend its severity and why it is incredibly important to consider the thought: "If I am living in habitual sexual sin, the Bible places a question mark over my eternal standing with the Lord."

From a practical perspective, this is difficult terrain to navigate because only God knows where a man truly is in his heart. What about the man who really seems to be fighting but is struggling to get free? What if he has had a legitimate conversion experience but is now dabbling with porn? At what point does a man cross the line into habitual sin rather than just lapsing in a moment of weakness? From a human perspective, there are no clear-cut answers to these questions. Therefore, it is critical that we keep our eyes focused on what the Scriptures are teaching us and avoid leaning on our own understanding in this battle. It is clear that the Bible is unequivocally against any form of sexual sin in the lives of God's people. In fact, according to the passages I cited, *pornography is sinful 100% of the time.*

SOUND THE ALARM!

I became familiar with tornado sirens when we first moved to the Midwest. Over the years, it has been a common occurrence to hear the eerie sound of sirens going off when the weather conditions are right. They are designed to warn people to find shelter as soon as possible because a tornado has either been spotted or is beginning to form. The city will sound the alarm as a warning, but how someone responds to it is their decision. Some people may not even be able to hear the alarm, due to loud music or deep sleep. Others may hear the sirens but disregard them as a "false alarm" or an unwelcome disturbance. But some will take the warning seriously and immediately take shelter. The approach people take in response to the alarms can literally determine their fate, whether life or death.

I hope that this chapter rings like a piercing siren to each man regarding the issue of sexual sin. I fear that some will hear the warnings of Scripture and brush them off as fanatical or misconstrued and fail to develop a sobriety about the truth regarding sexual sin and its dire consequences. My prayer is that every man who is reading this book will not only hear the alarm but allow the warning to cause them to seek shelter in the Lord.

The next chapter is going to discuss several of the main repercussions of allowing pornography into our lives.

CHAPTER 4

Refresh://defining-sin

PRAYER POINTS

- Pray that the Lord will give you a sobriety about the serious nature of sexual sin and reveal any excuses you are making for sin in your life

- Pray that the modern church will return to sincere teaching on holiness and purity

- Pray for protection from sexual temptation for specific men in your church, family and social circles

DISCUSSION QUESTIONS

1. Do you think that Paul's warning about disqualification in the Kingdom of God applies to a Christian man who looks at porn? Why or why not?

2. Do you find the statistics given about the modern church's permissive stance on pornography surprising? Why or why not?

3. Explain what it means in your own words to put to death your sinful nature. How can that principle apply to a man's battle with porn?

4. Can you think of other passages of Scripture that reference the dangers of sexual immorality? What is unique in those passages from the ones listed in this chapter?

5. In your past experience, how have you seen church discipline modeled? How is it the same or how does it differ from the way that Paul advised the Corinthians to deal with the sinning brother?

PERSONAL APPLICATION QUESTIONS

1. Based on your lifestyle, how serious have you taken the Scriptures in this chapter that forbid sexual sin in the life of a believer?

2. If you were to answer the Barna survey referenced in the beginning of the chapter, how would you respond regarding your attitude toward porn? Does that need to change based on the content of this chapter?

3. How have you tried to use Scriptural principles in the past to alleviate your sense of guilt or responsibility for sin?

5

Page Down:// the-consequences

THE BIBLE PLACES A HIGH PREMIUM ON wisdom. Entire books, such as Proverbs and Ecclesiastes, were written with the intent of imparting godly wisdom to all who will apply it. Proverbs 22:3 tells us, "A prudent person foresees danger and takes precautions. The simpleton goes blindly on and suffers the consequences." (NLT) This Scripture is warning that only fools fail to look ahead at potential dangers along their path. A wise man will take the consequences of his actions into account. Essentially, if our life story was recorded on a digital document, true wisdom involves hitting the Page Down button from time to time. It requires we consider the long-term effects of every action we take. Biblical wisdom should change a man's thinking from "What is going to feel the best at this moment?" to "Is this decision going to lead me where I want to be five years from now?"

The Apostle Paul picks up on this principle when he wrote about sowing spiritual seeds. In Galatians 6, he wrote:

Do not be deceived, God is not mocked; for whatever a man sows, that he will also reap. For he who sows to his flesh will of the flesh reap corruption, but he who sows to the Spirit will of the Spirit reap everlasting life. (vss. 7-8)

Paul uses a common farming metaphor to describe the effects of our actions. If we act in the interest of our flesh, we can expect a harvest of corruption in our lives. The Greek word for *corruption* is *phthorá* and it is defined as, "destruction from internal corruption, deterioration, decay."[1] I cannot think of a more accurate depiction of what happens to the internal world of the man who is given over to pornography. As he continues to sow seeds of sin into the soil of his heart, he begins to rot from the inside out.

This spiritual principle is immutable, and Paul does not offer exemption status to anyone. The law of sowing and reaping is one of God's spiritual laws and it applies to all of us. The harvest that comes from our actions is guaranteed. However, we do not get to choose the specific circumstances or timing of that harvest. If we sow to the Spirit, a harvest of everlasting life will manifest in our lives through the favor of God. His blessings will surely come in the way and timing that *He* chooses. In a similar way, if we sow seeds to the flesh, the harvest of corruption will come in a way and time that we cannot control. With that in mind, we will examine four principles of the spiritual harvest that will be reaped for *every* man who indulges in pornography.

HARVEST PRINCIPLE 1:

Pornography Causes a Moral Landslide

I remember the early years of my drug use, when I was regularly smoking marijuana, drinking alcohol and abusing "recreational" drugs. I always had a bias against cocaine, meth and heroin users. In my eyes, people involved in those drugs were the *real* addicts. I was just trying to have a good time with what I viewed as lesser substances, dismissing the idea that I was an addict myself. In my view, the addicts were the people who had lost everything due to their addiction. And I vowed to myself that I was *never* going to be one of them.

As the cycle of degradation led me deeper down the rabbit hole of addiction, I found myself experimenting with cocaine, just to see what all the fuss was about. That initial taste began the headfirst plunge that turned me into the exact person I was determined to never become. Within a couple of years, I had lost everything and found myself in circumstances I never imagined could happen to me.

I see the same concept in the world of pornography. Porn seeks to make perverse activity the normal expression of sexuality. As the years have passed, pornographic materials have become unimaginably obscene and twisted. A man might begin with less depraved material, like "softcore" porn and think, "I'll never get into anything harder than that." Then he slowly begins to dabble with darker content as the excitement of the gateway porn fades. He pushes the limits a little further, all the while thinking to himself, "I'll never get into _____." You can fill in the blank with any type of perversion you can imagine.

When someone is given over to viewing pornography, something happens in their internal world. What they once considered repulsive becomes increasingly acceptable and for many, eventually the thing they most desire. Many sex addicts will admit that the longer that they stayed in that lifestyle, the more depraved the sexual acts became. They simply thought they were going to have a little enjoyment, and they ended up imprisoned in a world of perversion and darkness.

Research backs this up, as one report states that people who consume increasing amounts of pornography tend to enjoy "degrading, uncommon, or aggressive sexual behaviors."[2] Those of us who have experienced the depths of porn addiction are all too familiar with the continuous pull into deeper perversion. I have often expressed my gratitude to the Lord that He set me free before smartphones were readily available. The ease of access and the ability to hide only makes the downhill slope that much quicker today. For those who are still in the grips of porn addiction, allow this principle to serve as a strong warning: Do not deceive yourself into thinking that you can somehow control this in your life!

At one point, every man who has destroyed his life with sexual sin thought that he could keep things "under control." Sin has a deceptive quality that causes a man to think that he is the one in the driver's seat. He assumes that he can decide how far he wants to go and that, at any time, he can stop and get out. But he often fails to consider that a seed of corruption has been planted by that sinful behavior. If we sow carnal seeds through pornography into our hearts, the harvest will include a moral landslide that will take us down a path of wickedness much further than we intended to go.

HARVEST PRINCIPLE 2:
Pornography Fuels Lust

One of the worst consequences a porn user experiences is how it turns both men and women into objects of lust. This is the complete opposite of God's design. While pleasure is a wonderful byproduct of marital sex, intimacy between a husband and wife is its main purpose. By contrast, viewing pornography is driven by pure lust. There is no true intimacy experienced between a man and the people he views in porn.

An interesting study was performed by Princeton and Stanford in which men were shown pictures of women fully clothed and other pictures of women barely clothed. The way that a man's brain responded to the stimuli is both informative and fascinating. The part of the brain that recognizes people's faces was activated *only* when looking at the clothed women. The conclusion was that the study "suggests that sexualized women are more closely associated with being the objects, not the agents, of action as compared to clothed women."[3]

This should be a disturbing thought to a Christian man. Anyone who has given over to pornography has found the objectification of other people to be an increasing issue in his life. To think that he can reprogram his brain to view women as objects rather than souls through repeated encounters with porn should be startling. This objectification makes the Christian life impossible to live out. As followers of Christ, we are commanded to love others. This theme is all throughout Scripture:

- You shall love your neighbor as yourself. **(Mark 12:31)**

- A new commandment I give to you, that you love one another; as I have loved you, that you also love one another. **(John 13:34)**

- This is My commandment, that you love one another as I have loved you. **(John 15:12)**

Pornography will render a man powerless to obey these commands. This is because it is impossible to love people and objectify them at the same time. Many might view hatred as the opposite of love. But in many ways, lust is also its spiritual antonym. The word *lust* Paul uses in Romans 1:27 when he talks about people "burning with lust" is *orexis*, and it means "desire, longing, craving."[4] It is describing a strong urge to appropriate something for oneself. While love is generous and giving; lust is greedy and taking. Love is focused on others, while lust is only concerned with self. Love is willing to sacrifice; lust is willing to compromise one's values to get what it wants. At the heart of lust is covetousness. Rex Andrews once described it as taking virtue from someone that does not belong to us.[5]

Pornography is like an incubator for lust in the heart of a man. It trains him to view people as objects for personal pleasure. And when a man's eyes are not staring at a screen, the same lust that fuels his habit will follow him to the grocery store, workplace and even church. Fantasy is a sinful habit that goes hand-in-hand with porn. A man will discover that he cannot control his eyes or his thoughts, and his whole world becomes filtered through that lustful lens.

Even long after pornography is deleted from a man's life, lust is something that shapes the way he views others. I believe the Lord will increasingly bring any man with a true desire for purity into greater levels of victory in this area. But it is counter-cultural, so he will have to learn how to continually fight. Every time you see a billboard with a swimsuit model or a tabloid with the hottest celebrities, you are faced with a cultural precedent that tells you to selfishly objectify people. Disciplining yourself to pray for others when you are tempted to lust is one effective way to shift your internal gears (more about this in Chapter 11).

Pornography is a sure-fire way to fuel a lustful heart. When we sow seeds of the flesh through porn, it will prevent us from being able to truly love as it centers our lives around our selfish desires.

HARVEST PRINCIPLE 3:
Pornography Blocks Contentment

"I thought that when I got married, this lust problem would go away."

It is not uncommon for men to assume that marriage is the perfect solution to their porn problem. Their logic is simple: "Since I have a sex problem, I need a marital relationship where I can have sex without guilt or shame." However, this line of thinking is based on faulty logic. Many porn addicts incorrectly view their struggle as a sex problem. That being the case, it stands to reason that getting married would solve it. However, the truth is that porn is not a sex problem; it is a sin problem rooted in the lust of the heart. This means that physical changes alone cannot fix the problem. Instead, a spiritual change is required.

Jesus tells us in Matthew 5:27-28: "You have heard that it was said to those of old, 'You shall not commit adultery.' But I say to you that whoever looks at a woman to lust for her has already committed adultery with her in his heart." He took this Old Testament commandment that focused on the outward action of adultery and shifted the focus to the root of the issue. Long before an adulterous act is committed, a person's heart is already given over to lust. Adultery is only the outward manifestation of a sinful heart. The same can be said of any other form of outward sexual sin. Before sin manifests through a man's outward actions, it has already taken root internally. In another passage, Jesus repeated this thought when He said, "For out of the heart come evil thoughts—murder, adultery, sexual immorality, theft, false testimony, slander."[6] The Bible is quite clear: sexual lust is a sin problem, and it is rooted in the heart of a man.

This is not to imply that being married has no impact on a lustful heart. Paul himself suggested that a man get married rather than burn with lust.[7] The point is that while marriage may provide an opportunity to have sexual relations without the guilt that accompanies masturbation or fornication, it cannot fix heart issues. Unfortunately, many discover that truth the hard way. After the excitement of the wedding ceremony and the honeymoon die off, a man finds that his lust is just as active as before he walked down the aisle. His fantasy life is thriving and he begins to long for sexual experiences that healthy marital relations will not provide. If it were true that marriage was enough to fix the problem, pornography and adulterous affairs would be rare amongst married couples. But as we all know, these issues are all too common nowadays. One study actually found that pornography use increases the marital infidelity rate by more than 300%.[8] Marital intercourse—although it is a blessing from God when it occurs in a pure loving relationship—will not satisfy a man's longing for the forbidden fruit of his fantasies.

I fell for this lie myself. Having been given over to pornography for many years, the root of lust in my heart was deeply entrenched. After failing to get free after many attempts, I comforted myself that it would all change when I got married. When I met my wife, I assured myself that my days in bondage to pornography were behind me. But it was not long into the marriage that I found my lust problem had followed me to the altar. No matter how sincere I thought I was when I recited my vows, that commitment alone was not enough to set me free. I wound up wasting many precious years of marriage in secret bondage, unable to escape the misery of sexual addiction. 1 Timothy 6:6 tells us that "godliness with contentment is great gain." Porn use will prevent a professing Christian from obtaining that kind of contentment.

I thank God that He is not only in the business of setting men free from sexual sin, but that He is willing and able to resurrect marriages that have been affected by it. But it is crucial to understand that the harvest of corruption that comes from pornography will create an appetite for sex that cannot be satisfied by marriage alone.

HARVEST PRINCIPLE 4:

Pornography Creates Victims

One of the biggest lies that men believe when they are hooked on porn is: "This isn't affecting anyone but me." However, that short-sighted perspective is based on a deceptive train of thought. Someone might rank pornography in a different category from other forms of sexual sin because it does not seem to directly involve other people. In reality, the victims of pornography are many and porn acts as a gateway to all the other forms of sexual sin.

Consider the manipulation, coercion, violence and trafficking that go hand-in-hand with porn production. Just because the actors and actresses might look like they are consenting to what is taking place, the reality is much darker than we want to imagine. Here are several shocking facts to contemplate:

- According to cases reported to the National Human Trafficking Hotline, pornography was ranked as the third most common form of sex trafficking.[9]

- The former Senior Advisor on Trafficking in Persons for the U.S. State Department (Laura Lederer) stated, "Pornography is a brilliant social marketing campaign for commercial sexual exploitation."[10]

- In one year, The Internet Watch Foundation assessed 132,676 URLs that they could confirm offered access to child sexual abuse imagery.[11]

- The International Association of Internet Hotlines "traced online child sexual abuse material to over 70 countries" in one year.[12]

- A former porn actress, Shelley Lubben, testified that, "Women are lured in, coerced and forced to do sex acts they never agreed to do…[and given] drugs and alcohol to help get through hardcore scenes."[13]

These are just a few examples of many studies that reveal the connection between the porn empire and the exploitation of adults and children. Not only that, but there is a clear link between porn and violence. Research has found:

Even by the lowest estimate…more than 1 in every 3 porn videos depicts sexual violence or aggression. In fact, according to a study that analyzed porn titles alone, 1 out of every 8 titles suggested to first-time users on porn sites described acts of sexual violence.[14]

With these statistics in mind, consider how many lives have been destroyed, not only inside the porn industry, but because of it.

- How many marriages have resulted in divorce because of porn, even as a by-product?

- How many children have been left without a mother or father in the home?

- How many babies have been aborted as a result of an unexpected pregnancy?

- How many people have walked through years of shame, trauma and torment because of being molested, raped or coerced?

- How many people have suffered from sexually transmitted diseases?

- How many men, women and children are currently being used as sex slaves today not only because of porn, but for the creation of it?

To claim that pornography is victimless is not only naïve but completely foolish. Perhaps if this dark side of porn was more broadly known, men would reconsider before clicking on that tempting web link.

The reality of the horrors of sexual trauma hit home to me on one occasion. My wife and I were training to become foster parents. The topic of one of the sessions was "Sexual Abuse." We both went into the session with the same thought: "Let's get this over with as quickly as possible." We had hopes that they would talk in generalities and that it would not become too graphic. Much to our dismay that hope quickly dissipated.

Our group project consisted of taking twelve pieces of paper out of an envelope and reading them. Each had a grotesquely descriptive action that an adult might do to a child. To be honest, it was horrifying. Our job as a group was to put the actions in order from most invasive to least invasive. When the teacher asked at the end, "How did that make you feel?" My wife replied, "Like vomiting." I shared her sentiment.

The trainer explained to us the purpose of the project. If we were to foster a child who opened up to us about being abused, we needed to be able to respond in a way that would not make the child see the shock on our faces. The hope was that by having us exposed to the concepts in a classroom ahead of time, we could avoid overreacting. But as we were going through the session, discussing unmentionable atrocities that occur to children every single day, there was something bothering me even deeper than the material itself. I could not put my finger on it exactly at the time, but I felt so incredibly dirty and shameful about my own past sexual sin. While my sin never involved children, I realized that I had still sought out, viewed, and lusted after probably every one of those actions on those twelve sheets of paper. Although I was not doing it in the same context (against children), I too shared an enjoyment of sexual perversion just like the perpetrators practiced.

Those of us who have viewed pornographic magazines or digital content, have contributed to the industry by showing an interest in it. Even "free" content is monitored to see what is most effective to reach the consumer. Think about it. If no one was interested in pornography, the industry would die overnight. We need to come to terms with the fact that our involvement in porn makes us complicit in destroying lives around the world. That is an arena that no Christian man should ever take part in.

Pornography will take a man where he does not want to go. Although many deceive themselves that they can control it, history reveals that sexual sin is a more powerful force than any man can contend with in his own strength. We need the power of God to set us free. If we are not reaping the type of harvest that we desire, it is because we have sown the wrong kinds of seed. Now, let us consider what it looks like to sow good spiritual seeds in the following chapters.

CHAPTER 5

Page Down:// the-consequences

PRAYER POINTS

- Pray for those who are being victimized in the porn industry right now as you are reading these words:

    * Pray that the darkness will be exposed and that those perpetrating the acts will come to Christ

    * Pray that the men and women who are doing the pornographic acts will have an encounter with Jesus

    * Pray for ministries that are actively providing help for victims of sex trafficking

DISCUSSION QUESTIONS

1. What are some of the unexpected consequences a man might face as he slides deeper into the moral depravity of porn?

2. If God was to forgive a man from porn and set him free, does that mean the consequences of his sin will also go away? Why or why not?

3. How does lust prevent a man from walking in the love of God?

4. Why does the chapter explain that marriage cannot fix a lust problem? Do you think this is a common misconception for many men?

5. How does a man's pursuit of porn help to fuel the sex-trafficking industry? Should this be a concern for a casual user of porn?

PERSONAL APPLICATION QUESTIONS

1. Which of the four points in this chapter hits closest to home in your own life?

2. What consequences have you experienced in your life as a result of porn spiritually, mentally, emotionally, relationally, financially and physically?

3. How has pornography affected your personal sense of contentment?

PART TWO:// the-decision

6

Scroll Lock:// the-solomon-spirit

KING SOLOMON WAS BORN INTO a royal family that had been deeply impacted by sexual sin. After an adulterous affair occurred between his parents, King David and Bathsheba, the two got married and had children. The first baby who was conceived during the affair had passed away shortly after his birth as a result of God's judgment for David's sin. After the infant's death, Scripture tells us that David "comforted Bathsheba his wife, and went in to her and lay with her. So she bore a son, and he called his name Solomon."[1]

The events surrounding Solomon's birth are complicated because of everything that took place in David's life. It would not be a stretch to assume that as Solomon grew older, he would have heard the story about how his mother and father had first met. It is difficult to keep family secrets like that under wraps, especially when you are part of a royal family. Plus, David had written Psalm 51 about his sexual sin as a public testimony of his repentance. Considering his unique situation, one would hope that Solomon would learn from his father's mistakes and not repeat them.

THE RISE AND FALL OF A KING

The story of Solomon starts off very promising. The Scriptures tell us that Solomon "loved the Lord, walking in the statutes of his father David..."[2] God appeared to the king in a dream and essentially gave him a blank check by offering him anything that he wanted. Yahweh was so pleased when the king requested wisdom to lead Israel, that He not only promised that Solomon would be the wisest man to ever live but also blessed him with riches and honor.[3] Under most of Solomon's reign, Israel lived in great prosperity and peace.[4] It seemed that he was going to follow in his father's footsteps as a man after God's own heart. Unfortunately, an attitude of compromise began to creep in.

In Deuteronomy, we are told that all kings were required to write out their own copy of the Torah for study. This would not only ensure that the leaders of Israel were familiar with the words of the Law, but it also provided a form of national accountability. In the Law are several clear boundaries aimed at helping kings avoid the temptation to use their power in ways that would cause their hearts to go astray. For example:

- Israel was forbidden to make treaties with the surrounding nations through marriage so that they would not be tempted to worship their gods. (**Exodus 34:15-16; Deuteronomy 7:1-4**)

- A king was not to multiply horses, silver, gold, or wives for himself. He was especially forbidden to purchase horses in Egypt. (**Deuteronomy 17:16-17**)

As Solomon's story progresses, we find evidence of compromise in each of these areas. It began with a treaty that he made with Pharaoh of Egypt, involving a marriage with his daughter.[5] While Egypt was not a nation specifically forbidden for intermarriage in the Torah, it fits the bill of an enemy nation that served other gods which could become a spiritual stumbling block. Solomon also began amassing chariots and horsemen, even importing horses from Egypt.[6] The king became incredibly wealthy through his business dealings, effectively storing up gold and silver for himself. When you read through the story of Solomon's reign, it seems that the king was simply developing his military and strengthening the economy, as would be expected. But what should have been more important to Solomon was that he would lead his people spiritually by living under the authority of God in heartfelt obedience to the Torah.

Instead, what we see taking place in this season of Solomon's life is a blatant disregard for God's commands. It seems that through all the fame, power and riches that he was experiencing, something had slipped in that caused him to compromise. Unfortunately, the blessing and favor in his life did not draw him closer to the Lord but created the perfect combination of factors to cause him to slip further down the path of compromise.

SOLOMON'S PATHETIC TESTIMONY

1 Kings 11:1-4 expresses what I believe to be one of the most pitiful testimonies of any person in Scripture. It records:

King Solomon, however, loved many foreign women besides Pharaoh's daughter- Moabites, Ammonites, Edomites, Sidonians and Hittites. They were from nations about which the Lord had told the Israelites, 'You must not intermarry with them, because they will surely turn your hearts after their gods.' Nevertheless, Solomon held fast to them in love. He had seven hundred wives of royal birth and three hundred concubines, and his wives led him astray. As Solomon grew old, his wives turned his heart after other gods, and his heart was not fully devoted to the Lord his God, as the heart of David his father had been. (NIV)

This passage reminds us about God's command to avoid marrying women from the surrounding cultures. But the word *nevertheless* reveals that King Solomon's response was to harden his heart to the Lord. He should have known the potential consequences of giving over to lust, not only from God's Word, but also from his family history. If any man should have been on high alert for potential struggles with lust, it would have been Solomon. But not only did he hold "fast to them in love," he gave his entire life to a pursuit of women that makes David's one time affair look like a tea party.

How Solomon juggled any kind of relationship with a thousand women baffles my mind. At any rate, it was a glaring disregard of what he had been taught. He cast off all restraint and became a king who sought his own pleasure above all else. It is important to point out that Solomon's downfall into sin did not take place overnight. It was a process that must have taken many years. But once he began to live for himself rather than Yahweh, he was on a one-way spiral into moral depravity. With that background in mind, I want to present three character flaws that precipitated the third king of Israel giving over to unrepentant sexual sin.

CHARACTER FLAW #1:
Solomon Had Unheeded Wisdom

What makes Solomon's story so exasperating is the unique advantage that he had over every other human being that has ever lived. When he asked God for wisdom in his first dream, the Lord responded by saying, "I have done according to your words; see, I have given you a wise and understanding heart, so that there has not been anyone like you before you, nor shall any like you arise after you."[7] Think about what that means. Yahweh told Solomon that he would be the wisest man who would ever live! That gift of wisdom was much greater than mental acuity; it was the ability to examine any given situation and know the best course of action to take based on its long-term repercussions.

There are multiple examples of Solomon's wisdom recorded in the Scriptures. One is when two women approached the king with an argument over who was the mother of a child. Solomon called for the baby's execution, and the true mother immediately said, "O my lord, give her the living child, and by no means kill him."[8] It was obvious to Solomon that the true mother was the one who would rather sacrifice her relationship with her own child than see him harmed. The Scriptures say about that event, "And all Israel heard of the judgment which the king had rendered; and they feared the king, for they saw that the wisdom of God was in him to administer justice."[9]

1 Kings 4 states that people from all over the earth came to listen to the wisdom of Solomon.[10] One of them was the queen of Sheba, who testified that his wisdom and prosperity exceeded her expectations.[11] In addition, Solomon was used by God to write many of the proverbs in the Bible that remain relevant today. These writings are filled with rich, practical advice and have been a source of blessing to innumerable people for three thousand years. Proverbs 5 is loaded with wisdom, warning men about the dangers of sexual sin. In that proverb, he wrote:

My son, pay attention to my wisdom; lend your ear to my understanding, that you may preserve discretion, and your lips may keep knowledge. For the lips of an immoral woman drip honey, and her mouth is smoother than oil; but in the end she is bitter as wormwood, sharp as a two-edged sword. Her feet go down to death, her steps lay hold of hell. (vss. 1-5)

Solomon implored men to beware of falling into the trap of sexual sin. He went on to give married men the following advice:

Let your fountain be blessed, and rejoice with the wife of your youth…always be enraptured with her love…For why should you, my son, be enraptured by an immoral woman, and be embraced in the arms of a seductress? (vss. 18-20)

He then closed the Proverb with the following warning:

For the ways of man are before the eyes of the Lord, and He ponders all his paths. His own iniquities entrap the wicked man, and he is caught in the cords of his sin. He shall die for lack of instruction, and in the greatness of his folly he shall go astray. (vss. 21-23)

The context of this proverb is about avoiding an immoral woman who is trying to lure a man into adultery. This is solid, godly wisdom that any man would do well to heed. However, considering these are the words of Solomon, the foolish way that he lived his life regarding sexual sin is appalling. His life became the very embodiment of a man who refused his own wisdom and "in the greatness of his folly," went astray. This should cause us to ask, "How could a man who had been blessed with such godly wisdom form a lifestyle that was such a contradiction to it?" The answer is that *having* wisdom and *heeding* wisdom are two entirely different matters.

Knowing how to apply wisdom does not necessarily guarantee a man will choose to walk in it. This reveals how preachers of righteousness can fall into sin themselves. Wisdom only adds value to the lives of those who choose to heed it. This also explains how a man who has access to the Bible, heard hundreds of sermons, read numerous Christian books, and even taught the wisdom of God can still foolishly become enslaved to pornography. James warned us about this danger when he wrote, "Be doers of the word, and not hearers only, deceiving yourselves."[12] It is not a lack of knowledge of right and wrong but his refusal to heed God's wisdom that causes a professing Christian to get entangled in sexual sin.

Through this book, you are being provided with godly wisdom on how to get free and stay free, but if you refuse to appropriate that wisdom, you will remain in bondage. Solomon apparently refused to heed his own gift of wisdom and suffered the consequences. Let me implore all of us as men of God to become *heeders* of the wisdom given to us in the Bible.

CHARACTER FLAW #2:
Solomon Had Unbridled Passions

Sexual lust was the root sin that enslaved King Solomon. As a man whose wisdom brought him near super-hero status, his lust for women proved to be his kryptonite. This is why it is so ironic that God used him to author the book we call "Song of Solomon." This book is a beautiful piece of literature that describes healthy sexual passion in the confines of marriage between a man and a woman. It was inspired by the Holy Spirit, but taking advice about romance from a man who had a thousand wives and concubines could be the textbook definition of irony.

Just the sheer logistics of forming any kind of relationship with that many women is mind-boggling, much less having marriages and sexual relations with each of them. Think about it. If Solomon held a wedding ceremony every day, it would have taken almost two years just to marry all his wives. This was a prolonged pursuit for Solomon, driven by lust and a greed for power, not a short season of bad decisions.

While it might be easy to stand back and judge Solomon's out-of-control appetite for sex, those of us who have been in bondage to pornography are not much different internally. Maybe we did not act out with women to that degree, but if you consider every pornographic picture or video as a sexual relationship, many of us would have far exceeded Solomon's sin. The only real difference is that he had the power and ability to fulfill his lustful desires, while we have been limited in resources and opportunity. Solomon's life merely illustrates what can happen if a man's fantasies become a reality.

What Solomon needed is what we also need: a bridle for our passions. A bridle is a tool used by horse riders to control these powerful animals. It connects a piece in the mouth of the horse to the reins that the rider holds in his hands. Although most men could never force a horse to go where it did not want to go, a simple tug on the reins in one direction or the other causes enough discomfort in a horse's mouth to get it to turn. A bridle provides a great illustration of what self-control is supposed to look like. As men of God, we are called to bridle our passions. If we refuse to do that, they will dictate the direction of our lives and cause us to go wherever our flesh desires.

The Scriptures are clear that it is up to us as men of God to take the reins in our battle with the flesh:

- Whoever has no rule over his own spirit is like a city broken down, without walls. **(Proverbs 25:28)**

- Therefore do not let sin reign in your mortal body, that you should obey it in its lusts. **(Romans 6:12)**

- Walk in the Spirit, and you shall not fulfill the lust of the flesh. **(Galatians 5:16)**

- Let your conduct be without covetousness; be content with such things as you have. **(Hebrews 13:5)**

Imagine if Solomon's wisdom had led him to embrace his personal responsibility for self-control and contentment in his life. What if Pharaoh's daughter had been enough for him? What if he truly understood the dangers of casting off all restraint? His story could have turned out much differently if he had just been willing to bridle his passions. Thomas à Kempis wrote:

"True peace of heart is found in resisting passions, not in satisfying them. There is no peace in the carnal man, in the man given to vain attractions, but there is peace in the fervent and spiritual man."[13]

Through the process of repentance, the Lord will give the sincere man a fresh desire for self-control and true contentment, as well as the grace to put it into practice. However, if we refuse to repent, we will continue to be slaves to our passions just like Solomon was to his.

CHARACTER FLAW #3:
Solomon Had an Unsubmitted Will

The third aspect of Solomon's life is the root of all the problems he experienced. In many ways, he had the world at his fingertips. However, because of his unwillingness to obey God, he ended up entangled in sin and ultimately fell away from the Lord.

While many will be familiar with the first time God appeared to Solomon when He promised to bless him, He also appeared to him a second time in a lesser-known dream. This happened after the construction of the Temple had been completed. However, this time, there was a different tone in God's words to Solomon:

"Now if you walk before Me as your father David walked, in integrity of heart and in uprightness, to do according to all that I have commanded you, and if you keep My statutes and My judgments, then I will establish the throne of your kingdom over Israel forever, as I promised David your father, saying, 'You shall not fail to have a man on the throne of Israel.' But if you or your sons at all turn from following Me, and do not keep My commandments and My statutes which I have set before you, but go and serve other gods and worship them, then I will cut off Israel from the land which I have given them; and this house which I have consecrated for My name I will cast out of My sight…" (**1 Kings 9:4-7**)

When I read this passage, I have to ask, "Why did God feel it was necessary to bring that kind of warning to Solomon?" It is as if He is saying, "Watch out! I see something in your life that has the potential to destroy you." During the duration between the two dreams, I think the Lord could see a dangerous passion for worldly status and pleasure forming in the heart of this king.

Solomon contributed another book to the Bible called Ecclesiastes. Its theme is essentially that true satisfaction, peace and purpose can only be found in one's relationship with the Lord and not in anything this world has to offer. What is fascinating to me is that, throughout the book, Solomon writes about all the ways that he intentionally tried to seek fulfillment in this world. He threw himself fully into many pursuits, including wisdom (1:12-18), pleasure (2:1-11), work (2:17-26), relationships (4:1-12), status (4:13-16) and riches (5:8-6:12). At the very end of his life, he finally came to see how much grief he had brought upon himself by disobeying God's commandments.

Solomon could not declare himself to be ignorant of the Torah. As stated earlier, one of the requirements of Israel's kings from Deuteronomy 17:18-20 states:

Also it shall be, when he sits on the throne of his kingdom, that he shall write for himself a copy of this law in a book…And it shall be with him, and he shall read it all the days of his life, that he may learn to fear the Lord his God and be careful to observe all the words of this law and these statutes, that his heart may not be lifted above his brethren, that he may not turn aside from the commandment to the right hand or to the left...

Solomon would have handwritten his own personal copy of the Law and fully understood that it forbade his marriages as well as his military and economic pursuits. The story of Solomon is a heartbreaking tale of a life wasted on selfish living. His unique potential to live for the Lord placed him in a category all his own. His accountability to the truth is demonstrated through the three books of the Bible that he helped author. His life displays a man who knew what God wanted yet stubbornly refused to obey. This is why 1 Kings 11 says that Solomon "loved many foreign women" and "clung to these in love."[14]

The word for *clung* in Hebrew is *dabaq*, which means, "held fast, cling, cleave to...sometimes with idea of physical proximity retained."[15] Solomon's lust was so powerful that he held on tightly and refused to let go, even though God had clearly said, "No." This death-grip on sexual sin is what caused him to do his will instead of the Lord's. The Living Bible translates it this way:

...even though the Lord had clearly instructed his people not to marry into those nations, because the women they married would get them started worshiping their gods. Yet Solomon did it anyway. (1 Kings 11:2)

God can see the direction that our decisions will take us. The Holy Spirit will convict and warn the man who is dabbling with lustful thoughts and urges about the consequences of acting on them. Ultimately, however, a man must approach God's instruction with sincere obedience if he is going to avoid the inevitable downfall. It all comes down to whether he will choose to obey his own will or God's.

THE SOLOMON SPIRIT

I chronicled Solomon's story because I see so many similarities in the lives of Christians who are involved in pornography. Just like Solomon, most Christian men are well aware of the commandments of Scripture regarding sexual sin. For most men in the church, it is not an issue of knowledge. I have never counseled a Christian involved with pornography, showed him verses about sexual immorality, and had him say, "Oh. I'm so glad you showed me those passages. I had no idea that sexual immorality is a sin." Although the world often tries to promote pornography in a positive light, this is not the typical attitude of most Christian men I talk to. They are aware of the detrimental effect it has on their spiritual life and their family. If they really believed that it was a healthy habit, they would not be putting so much effort into hiding it. The guilt and shame that they feel about it should be an indicator that something is wrong.

Despite the clear warnings of Scripture and the known consequences that their sin is causing, they "hold fast in love" to their treasured sin just like Solomon did. I call this attitude the Solomon Spirit. His lifestyle spoke the following message: "Even though I know sexual sin is wrong; even though I have seen its effects in the lives of other people; even though I've been warned by God to avoid it, I'm going to do it anyway because I love it." Solomon represents men who understand the consequences of sexual sin yet still pursue it. They are men who will not heed wisdom, bridle their passions or submit their will to the Lord.

When I speak to a group of men about pornography, it is this type of attitude that I attempt to come against. The greatest obstacle I see for Christians is this stubborn refusal to do whatever it takes to be free. So many will nod their heads and say, "Amen" to the things that are being expressed, but so few are willing to do anything about them. If this describes your attitude, I pray that the Lord will help you to overcome the Solomon Spirit before it is too late.

SOLOMON'S FINAL CHAPTER

Solomon's story ends on a tragic note. God brought judgment upon the nation through adversaries He raised up against Israel, ending the season of peace they had enjoyed. The Lord took away ten of the tribes from Solomon's leadership and gave them to a man named Jeroboam. Solomon then attempted to kill this man even though he was anointed by the Lord for the task. Then his tragic story ends in his death.[16]

One can see the great excitement building like a crescendo at the beginning of Solomon's leadership over the nation. But because of his attitude and actions, his story ended in a very anticlimactic way:

> For it was so, when Solomon was old, that his wives turned his heart after other gods; and his heart was not loyal to the Lord his God...Solomon did evil in the sight of the Lord, and did not fully follow the Lord, as did his father David...So the Lord became angry with Solomon, because his heart had turned from the Lord God of Israel, who had appeared to him twice, and had commanded him concerning this thing, that he should not go after other gods; but he did not keep what the Lord had commanded.
> **(1 Kings 11:4, 6, 9-10)**

The story of King Solomon has been written and recorded in the annals of history. How our story will be written is going to be determined by how we walk through a process of repentance that the Lord desires for us. Regardless of what Solomon decided, the questions that need to be answered now are: Will *you* heed the wisdom being offered? Will *you* do what it takes to get your passions under control? Will *you* follow the will of God into freedom, or follow the desires of your flesh into deeper bondage? The choice is yours to make. May the Lord grant each of you reading these words the ability to bend your knee at the cross and choose His way rather than your own.

In the next chapter, Solomon's father will show us what it looks like to deal with sexual sin God's way.

CHAPTER 6

Scroll Lock:// the-solomon-spirit

PRAYER POINTS

- Pray that the owners, managers and executives who control the porn industry will have "Saul of Damascus" experiences and truly encounter Christ

- Pray for protection from pride and temptation for your church's leadership team

- Pray that the Lord will soften your heart and give you the desire to submit your will to His

DISCUSSION QUESTIONS

1. How does Solomon's slow fade relate to the life of a believer who is in sexual sin?

2. Find some Scriptures not listed in the chapter that speak about self-control and contentment. What do these passages add to the conversation about bridling our wills?

3. What are three practical actions that Solomon could have taken that might have turned the trajectory of his life toward God?

4. How did compromise in other areas contribute to Solomon's sexual sin?

5. How does Solomon's life resemble a professing Christian who looks at porn?

PERSONAL APPLICATION QUESTIONS

1. Based on the three character qualities of Solomon's life given in the chapter, which do you see playing out in your life? How can you take steps to change in that area?

2. What other areas in your life do you see compromise other than pornography?

3. Solomon's story ended on a tragic note. If someone were writing a biography about your life, what are three qualities you hope they will use to describe you?

Alt://after-gods-own-heart

LTHOUGH FAMILIAR TO MOST CHRISTIANS, the life of King David is worth revisiting frequently for the faith lessons we can glean. His story is one of epic proportions. Singlehandedly slaying a bear and lion would be an impressive feat in itself,[1] but David went on to take down a giant that had the entire trained military of Israel petrified.[2] He experienced years of King Saul hunting him down with the intent to kill him.[3] Through it all he showed himself to be a man mighty in battle and respected as a strong leader even before his ascension to the throne.[4] David is one of the most revered kings of Israel, known for his extravagant sacrifices, military conquests and unhindered worship of Yahweh.

Yet, there was a time during David's reign when he allowed himself to become too comfortable, and it led to the biggest moral failure of his life. It is noteworthy that 2 Samuel 11:1 tells us that the incident occurred "at the time when kings go out to battle." David, the warrior king, should have been participating in battle with the soldiers in his army. Instead, he was taking it easy at the palace while his men were giving their lives on the battlefield. This lackadaisical attitude provided the perfect atmosphere for a major spiritual attack. If David could have known in advance what would transpire in the following weeks and months, perhaps he would have preferred fighting the natural battle, rather than entering the spiritual battlefield on the horizon of his life.

DAVID'S BIG MISTAKES

Whether David had ever seen Bathsheba before that day, we are not told. The Bible lays out the facts rather plainly. David was on the palace roof, Bathsheba was bathing within his eyesight, and David decided that he wanted her. Finding her attractive was not a sin. In fact, God designed his body with a sex drive, just like you and me. It was His idea that we find the opposite sex attractive, and yes, even to desire them sexually. However, along with that desire comes the responsibility of keeping oneself within the confines of God's boundaries. Rather than fleeing from temptation, he allowed his carnal curiosity to compel him to ask someone about her. That was Mistake #1: He put action to the lust in his heart and made this inquiry.

Even if Bathsheba had been single, seeing a woman naked and finding her attractive is no noble reason to call for her. In fact, that would be classified as a very inappropriate motive for wanting to have a woman come to your palace. This lust-charged thinking should have been a strong warning signal for this godly king. Making the situation even more deplorable was that he continued to toy with the idea of having sex with her even after confirming her identity and *marital status*. So, not only was David guilty of fishing for information about a woman based on her anatomy, but now he knew for sure that she belonged to another man.

I wonder how long it took before he called for her. It could have been minutes or hours; we do not know. What we do know is that David, the king known for winning major military battles, experienced a colossal defeat to temptation that day. The man who slayed Goliath with a slingshot could not overpower his internal passions. Verse 4 says, "Then David sent messengers, and took her." This is Mistake #2, and one that would cost him more than he could ever have imagined at that moment.

The following sequence of events seems to progress like clockwork. The king brought the object of his desire into the palace and slept with her. I have often wondered how it all transpired. Was Bathsheba so enamored with his position that she gave in without question? Did he abuse his position to force himself on her? While those details are not important in the grand scheme of things, my mind tends to ask the unanswered questions in the text. Either way, after the culmination of his lust, David sent Bathsheba home. Everything seemed to have gone according to David's plans…

THE CONSEQUENCES

The saga continued when Bathsheba ended up pregnant. Back when the king first satisfied his lust for her, I doubt a baby was on his radar. He was caught up in the moment, like any man driven by his desires. His goal was to commit the act that he was obsessing over, and long-term repercussions are rarely considered in the heat of the moment.

King David received news of the pregnancy and immediately moved into damage control mode. Rarely are good decisions made when people are dealing with a crisis. We can tell from David's reaction that he had one goal in mind: self-protection. We see no sign of a repentant heart. Instead, David was hell-bent on saving face. That becomes obvious when he gets her husband, Uriah, drunk in the hopes of getting him to sleep with her. All of this was done in an effort to pretend—at least for a while—that the baby belonged to Uriah. I suppose the truth would have come out eventually when the child looked nothing like Bathsheba's husband as it grew older, but David was not thinking long-term. He was trying to cover up his sin. "Desperate times call for desperate measures," he probably told himself.

I can relate to David's story because I also went to great lengths to keep my sin from discovery. How many of us have done something similar by deleting our browsing history, hiding pictures and video files in obscure places and using hidden apps and private browsers to avoid detection? What David did is no different than porn addicts today. He was deceived by thinking that removing all evidence of his sin could somehow make it go away.

In his scheme to cover his tracks, David did not take Uriah's integrity into account. Despite being intoxicated, he refused to sleep in the comfort of his bed with his beautiful wife because his fellow soldiers were out on the battlefield. This deepened David's dilemma. In his desperation, he made yet another horrible mistake when he devised a plan to make sure that Uriah ended up dead in battle. Maybe David felt like he would not be guilty of murder if it was the enemy who did the killing. I can only imagine how he attempted to rationalize his sin.

Unfortunately, David's plan was executed with precision. Uriah was slain in battle and his blood was on David's hands. The king was digging the hole of his moral depravity deeper and deeper. That one temptation on the rooftop had progressed from lust to adultery to murder. He then took Bathsheba in as his wife and probably breathed a sigh of relief when the wedding ceremony was finished. Finally, he could put the whole debacle behind him and move on.

His relationship with God must have been suffering severely at this point. One cannot commit such brazen acts of sin and remain close to the Lord. The shepherd boy who once found such delight in Yahweh had now turned his back on Him. David still needed to fulfill his royal responsibilities, which involved reading the Law, offering sacrifices and putting on a great religious show. Remember, his one goal was self-protection, so if he revealed that he was totally hardened to God, people would suspect something was wrong. However, inside, his heart had become callous as he refused to bring his sin into the light. So, the Lord called in reinforcements, namely a prophet named Nathan.

THE BIG MOMENT

The day came when Nathan appeared before the king and confronted him with a parable about injustice. He told a story about a rich man who stole a treasured lamb from his impoverished neighbor when a traveler had come to visit. Rather than offering a lamb from his own large flock to feed him, he slaughtered his neighbor's lamb. What made the situation even worse was that it was also his beloved pet. As King David heard the words of Nathan's story, his blood began to boil. In fact, Scripture says his anger was "greatly aroused against the man."[5] David made the following judgment: "As the Lord lives, the man who has done this shall surely die! And he shall restore fourfold for the lamb, because he did this thing and because he had no pity."[6] Nathan then replied in a tense moment that matches any dramatic climax Hollywood could create. He looked at the king—probably swallowing hard—and declared, "You are the man!"

We know very little about the personality of Nathan. However, his confrontation with David required great courage and a determination to do the will of God despite the possible consequences. Nathan was probably imagining what it might feel like if his head was separated from his shoulders by the executioner. Still, he continued with his rebuke:

> "Thus says the Lord God of Israel: 'I anointed you king over Israel, and I delivered you from the hand of Saul. I gave you your master's house and your master's wives into your keeping, and gave you the house of Israel and Judah. And if that had been too little, I also would have given you much more! Why have you despised the commandment of the Lord, to do evil in His sight? You have killed Uriah the Hittite with the sword; you have taken his wife to be your wife, and have killed him with the sword of the people of Ammon. Now therefore, the sword shall never depart from your house, because you have despised Me, and have taken the wife of Uriah the Hittite to be your wife.'" **(2 Samuel 12:7-10)**

Although this message was a sharp reproof from Yahweh, you can also detect a hint of grief in His words. The Lord reminded David that he had been promoted to the highest position in the nation by God Himself. He then told David that if all His blessings on the king's life had not been enough, He would have been willing to give him much more. However, despite the favor and authority that David had received, he still allowed his lust to drive him to commit adultery and murder. Essentially, the core of the message was, "Why would you do something like that after all that I have done for you?"

This rebuke could have elicited one of two responses in King David. First, he could have hardened his heart in pride and refused to listen to what Nathan was communicating. If he had rejected the rebuke, it would have opened his heart to further spiritual deception. There is no telling where that path would have led him. Second, he could humbly acknowledge his sin and repent. Fortunately for the king, he responded with these words: "I have sinned against the Lord."[7]

Perhaps this would be a good place to point out that David could have repented back before he even inquired about Bathsheba. He could have said, "Lord, I'm really struggling. That woman is very attractive, and I just saw her completely naked. I'm having an extremely difficult time with lustful thoughts. Please help me." No doubt the Lord would have answered that prayer and provided him with a way out. Maybe it would have awakened his sense of duty, and he would have joined his men in battle where he belonged.

David certainly had a chance to repent before he pursued adultery as well. He could have told the Lord, "Forgive me for my sin. I sent a messenger to find out who that woman was because I was attracted to her. Now I find out that she's married! Help me to do the right thing." David could have gotten out of it with two words to his servant: "Never mind." That would have been the end of it.

He had another opportunity to repent even when Bathsheba arrived at the palace. There had to be some kind of interaction in which he could have told her, "Forgive me. I should have never had you come here. This isn't right. You are married. Please go home and forget this ever happened."

At each stage of his sin, the stakes grew higher and the consequences greater. Along with that, his heightened lust was growing as well as his willingness to take risks to fulfill it. Rather than confining his sin to lustful thoughts, he ended up having to repent for adultery and murder as well. A woman lost her husband, an army lost a loyal soldier, and eventually the baby he and Bathsheba conceived lost its life. All of this happened as a result of David giving in to his lust. Those are serious consequences, and it was only the mercy of God that David was given a chance to repent.

Despite David's failure to cry out to the Lord before he committed adultery with Bathsheba, Yahweh revealed His longsuffering nature by reaching out to him through Nathan. Once he was confronted, David did not deny his sin or respond in anger. Neither did he make excuses or try to keep his sin covered. Instead, he did something beautiful in God's sight… he chose to repent. In the next chapter, we will discuss David's process of repentance as revealed in Psalm 51. Here, I want to explore what was true about his heart that caused him to repent when he was confronted by the Lord.

A MAN AFTER GOD'S OWN HEART

Scripture reveals a significant quality about David's heart early in his story. Back when Saul was still the reigning king, Yahweh had to remove him from the throne because of his continual disobedience. God sent the prophet Samuel to relay the following message to the disgraced king:

> "But now your kingdom shall not continue. The Lord has sought for Himself a man after His own heart, and the Lord has commanded him to be commander over His people, because you have not kept what the Lord commanded you." **(1 Samuel 13:14)**

The man that the Lord was referring to through this prophetic word was none other than David. Think about the implications of that statement. God described David as a man after His own heart even knowing in advance about the sin that he would one day commit. This thought is echoed when Paul recounted the story of David in Acts:

> "And when He had removed [Saul], He raised up for them David as king, to whom also He gave testimony and said, 'I have found David the son of Jesse, a man after My own heart, who will do all My will.'" **(Acts 13:22)**

No where else in Scripture is a man given this description other than

David. This has caused many to grapple with the question: "How could God describe someone who committed such an egregious sin a man after His own heart?" After reading the story about David and Bathsheba, one might assume that his legacy would be one of sinful disobedience, like many other kings recorded in Scripture. You might suppose that David had disqualified himself for leadership in the eyes of Yahweh. Instead, King David is referenced throughout the Bible with reverence and honor. How is it that he was able to recover from his sin and be restored in his relationship with God? The answer to that question should be of immense importance to any man who professes Christ yet has a history of pursuing sexual sin. I want to highlight three qualities about David that can become game changers for the man who truly desires to get free from porn.

QUALITY #1:
David Responded in Humility

The process of repentance that David experienced was not his only or even his easiest option. After all the work he had done to hide his sin, David could have kept his reputation intact by silencing Nathan. Doing so would have been a relatively simple process for the king of Israel. That might seem far-fetched, but David was already guilty of murdering one man to cover up his tracks. Also, the Bible contains several stories of kings arresting, imprisoning and even taking the life of God's prophets.[8] Take for example an event from the Gospels when a prophet called John the Baptist confronted a Jewish king:

> For Herod himself had sent and laid hold of John, and bound him in prison for the sake of Herodias, his brother Philip's wife; for he had married her. Because John had said to Herod, "It is not lawful for you to have your brother's wife." (**Mark 6:17-18**)

This situation between Herod and John had many parallels to David and Nathan. Each involved a confrontation between a prophet and a king regarding sexual sin. However, in the case of John the Baptist, King Herod not only had him imprisoned for his rebuke but even beheaded him. A similar response was within David's power. Fortunately for Nathan, it was not within the king's heart. While Herod responded with pride and self-preservation, David responded with humility. This is the kind of response that one would expect from a man after God's own heart. Ultimately, David chose the more difficult route of owning up to his sin and cleaning up his mess. His response kept him from digging his hole even deeper. In doing so, he displayed a humbleness of heart that all men need when they are confronted for their sin.

The Bible teaches in James 4:6, "God resists the proud, but gives grace to the humble." Yahweh would have resisted David if he had allowed pride to rise in his heart. Instead, he became the recipient of a massive display of God's mercy because of his humility. Any man who desires to find true freedom from sexual sin must foster this type of humble attitude. If we respond to the Lord's rebuke with arrogance, pride or indifference, we will keep the only One who can set us free at arm's length. Hopefully you understand by now that God is your only hope of getting out of your mess. If the pathway to His grace is humility, you need to humble yourself before the Lord, crying out for His mercy.

Unfortunately, King Solomon's story reveals that he lacked the humility of his father. Although the Bible does not explicitly state that Solomon was driven by pride, his refusal to obey the commands of the Torah is evidence that he was driven by selfish motives. His indulgent lifestyle and lavish living are qualities of a life consumed with pride. You could say of Solomon that he was "a man after his own heart" rather than the Lord's.

What is your internal response as you are reading through these stories? Are you trying to justify or minimize the fact that you are regularly viewing porn? Or are you allowing the conviction of the Holy Spirit to convince you that you cannot do this without His help? If you will respond to the Lord with humility—taking responsibility for your sin and turning to Him for help—David's story can become your story as well.

QUALITY #2:
David Submitted to God's Will

While Solomon displayed an unbroken will, David's reaction was much different. When Nathan confronted him, the prophet not only exposed his sin but also told him about the consequences that would result. The most heartbreaking news must have been that David and Bathsheba's baby would not live. When the baby became ill, David fasted and sought the Lord in desperation. He was hoping to get Yahweh to intervene and spare the life of his child. Nevertheless, the baby died seven days later. His servants were afraid to tell him the news, but David caught wind that something had taken place. When the child's death was reported to him, 2 Samuel 12:20 says that David "arose from the ground, washed and anointed himself, and changed his clothes; and he went into the house of the Lord and worshiped." In doing so, he displayed a heart that was surrendered to the will of God. Rather than getting upset with the Lord or demanding his own way, he worshiped despite the painful consequences he was experiencing.

I have witnessed the tragic outcome of men who seem to experience repentance, only to grow angry toward the Lord when they face the consequences of their sin. They had high hopes that God was going to spare them from repercussions such as divorce, job loss or a prison sentence. When their circumstances did not turn out the way they desired, they hardened themselves, proving that their repentance was not genuine. David had the opposite attitude. Even when he did not receive the miracle that he hoped for, he did not allow his disappointment to cause him to turn away from the Lord.

This is a challenging reality to face for the man who wants to delete porn from his life. In spite of experiencing genuine repentance, it is still possible that a man's sin could set a series of consequences into motion involving personal, relational, professional and legal hardships. The man who sincerely desires to repent must be willing to trust the Lord and have the same resolve David showed to submit to the will of God.

While many have experienced much harsher consequences for their sin, my repentance was not free of difficulties. My wife and I lost our ministry on the mission field when we were forced to resign. My credentials were placed on hold, and I was not allowed to do any ministry for a period of two years. Even after suffering all of that, I still refused to repent, almost losing my marriage in the process. Eventually, I embraced the process of repentance, but it cost me a year away from my family. My oldest daughter took her first steps while I was in the Pure Life Ministries Residential Program. My sin robbed me of experiencing many other precious moments with my family. However, I had to make the choice to allow God to have His way and to trust Him with the process.

Many men refuse to bring their sin into the light because they know what the consequences of it might entail. However, the severity of the consequences will only increase the longer they resist repentance. Is continuing to live a lie in order to avoid a potential divorce really a better option? Is staying in sin to protect a career or ministry a worthwhile trade? Of course not. A man must trust God with the foreseen and unforeseen circumstances. David was willing to submit himself to the will of God because he was a man after God's own heart.

QUALITY #3:

David Chose Change

A *desire* to change is not always followed by a *decision* to change. Any man can want to stop looking at porn—even to the point of desperation. But desire alone does not make him different from others who are unable to get free. David's story provides a worthy example of a man who made the decision to change, regardless of the cost. The king could have just responded to Nathan's rebuke with feelings of shame, guilt or self-pity. However, if his reaction remained on the level of emotions, it would not have resulted in freedom. He also took the actions necessary to bring about real change.

I have ministered to many addicts over the years and have found that many were unwilling to do the difficult work of cleaning up the mess they had made of their lives. They found the process to be too painful, uncomfortable and inconvenient. However, I have often asked them, "Would you rather have the pain of change or the pain of staying the same?"

Too often, people in habitual sin have a desire to get out of their painful circumstances but refuse to take the practical steps required to change. Repentance is more than an emotional response or a strong desire; it is a series of practical steps. The encouraging aspect of repentance is that you do not need to fight this battle by yourself. God is willing to join in your struggle and help you clean up the mess, but this is a decision you must make for yourself.

There are some aspects of our lives that we can choose to change through sheer willpower. Being more disciplined with exercise, watching our diet or pursuing an education are examples of this. However, the process of repentance is not something that we can do alone. Rather, it requires cooperation with the principles of God's Word and the power of the Holy Spirit. There are specific actions that we can take to position our hearts to receive a breakthrough in the spiritual realm, which I will detail in the next two sections of the book. Each action requires a choice to embrace change. The wonderful thing is that, once we take a step in that direction, the door is opened for the grace and transformative power of God to come rushing into our situation. Repentance involves stepping through a series of specific actions that allow God to bring us into freedom.

The level of the genuineness of your personal resolve to change is going to be revealed by what you do in response to the principles provided in the remainder of this book. They will place challenges in your path that you must navigate. Following the provided steps will require you to have conversations you probably do not want to have, exposing the darkest areas of your life to other people. It will also bring about drastic lifestyle changes. Whether you will follow-through like David or remain the same like Solomon is yet to be revealed.

The tragedy of Solomon's story is that he chose to dig his heels in, holding tightly to his flesh-driven lifestyle. There is no evidence that he ever changed. David, on the other hand, made the decision to change his course of action. He could have hardened his heart toward the Lord, rejecting his offer of restoration and living the rest of his days for himself. However, he opened the door to his heart and allowed the Lord to meet him in his mess. All men who desire freedom must do the same.

HOPE FOR A DIFFERENT FUTURE

What happened in David's life should be a source of great hope to the man stuck in pornography. It reveals that even a major moral failure does not have to permanently mark a man's life. Even though he slept with a married woman and arranged for her husband's death, David's legacy supersedes those tragic events. His season in sin was only for a relatively short period of his life because he repented. He went on to be honored as one of Israel's greatest kings, who—despite major sinful decisions—lived out his days for the glory of God. In fact, Jesus, the Son of God, was not ashamed to be referred to as "the son of David."[9]

Moving past moral failure and into a life that is pleasing to God can be your testimony as well. Your season of bondage in sexual sin began when the door was opened to porn in your life. However, because of repentance, you have an opportunity to see it come to an end, once and for all. It all comes down to the quality of your heart and how you choose to respond to the Lord's invitation. Each of us needs to follow David's example of humility, surrender to God's will and decide to go through the hard process of change.

In the next chapter, we are going to take a deeper look at the process of repentance that ultimately changed everything for him.

CHAPTER 7

Alt:// after-gods-own-heart

PRAYER POINTS

- Pray for people in your life that you know have been personally impacted by sexual sin, including those that have been affected by your own

- Pray that the Lord will grant you repentance and cause you to turn to Him in this season of your life

- Pray that local, state and national government officials will pass legislation that will limit the reach of pornography in our society

DISCUSSION QUESTIONS

1. When the Bible calls David a "man after His own heart," do you find this hard to believe knowing what he did with Bathsheba and her husband, Uriah? Why or why not?

2. Describe in your own words what you think it means that "God resists the proud."

3. Looking at David's life as a whole (from a shepherd boy to the king of Israel), what other examples can you find that show his heart for God?

4. What are the key differences between David's story and his son, Solomon's?

5. What makes the difference between men who embrace change in a way that leads to transformation and those that desire it but never actually change? How can a man ensure that he experiences the former?

PERSONAL APPLICATION QUESTIONS

1. Which of the three character qualities of David's life from the chapter do you need the most in your own?

2. David's story reveals how lust can spin out of control, leading to other sins, such as adultery and murder. How has lust done this in your life?

3. What can you do to move from desiring change to choosing change?

Return:// freedom-begins-here

PSALM 51 IS POSSIBLY THE GREATEST repentance prayer ever recorded. The subtitle of this psalm informs us that David wrote these words specifically after he repented of his sin with Bathsheba. By recording his supplications, he enabled future generations to see what took place in his heart when he finally humbled himself to the Lord. His prayer reveals the qualities of a truly repentant heart. In this chapter, we will examine David's prayer and highlight eight principles of true repentance.

REPENTANCE PRINCIPLE #1:
We Need God's Mercy

"Have mercy upon me, O God, according to Your lovingkindness;
According to the multitude of Your tender mercies." (vs. 1a)

The Hebrew word for *lovingkindness* in this verse is from the root word *checed*. This is a theologically rich term that refers to God's covenant love.[1] When David came face-to-face with the sinful condition of his heart, he knew there was only one thing he could do: throw himself on the mercy of Yahweh. The Bible tells us that:

- God is rich in mercy. **(Ephesians 2:4)**

- The Lord is gracious and full of compassion, slow to anger and great in mercy. **(Psalms 145:8)**

- All the paths of the Lord are mercy. **(Psalm 25:10)**

- Through the Lord's mercies we are not consumed, because His compassions fail not. **(Lamentations 3:22)**

- God shows mercy to thousands, to those who love Him and keep His commandments. **(Exodus 20:6)**

Mercy is more than something God does, it is part of His nature. David also used the term *tender mercies* (*racham*), which speaks of Yahweh's rich compassion for His people.[2] This Hebrew word can be translated *womb*, which "denotes a deep, tender compassion or mercy, often akin to the love a parent has for a child."[3] Those who approach the Lord with a sincere, humble heart, will find that He is compassionate, merciful and loving like a good father to His beloved child. David appealed to those qualities of God's nature, realizing his merciful Lord was his only hope for freedom.

This is the type of attitude that any man must have who wants to delete porn from his life. He needs to throw himself upon God's mercy rather than turning to the world for answers. The Lord is full of mercy and compassion toward us. He desires us to be free even more than we do. Because of this, we can approach Him with the confidence that He is willing to forgive and restore even the most broken of sinners. In fact, Psalm 147:11 states, "The Lord takes pleasure in those who fear Him, in those who hope in His mercy."

REPENTANCE PRINCIPLE #2:

Sin Must Be Confessed

"Blot out my transgressions. Wash me thoroughly from my iniquity, and cleanse me from my sin." (vss. 1b-2)

David used three different Hebrew words to speak of his offense against God. Each has its own unique connotation. The root word of *transgressions* is *pesha* and has to do with the violation of a law or command.[4] David had broken multiple commands in his pursuit of Bathsheba. *Iniquity* (*avon*) is the concept of twistedness or perversion.[5] It is an apt description of how sexual sin takes God's gift of sex and contorts it into a selfish, lust-driven act devoid of true love. The word *sin* (*chatta'ah*) has the connotation of falling short or missing the mark.[6] Just like David, every man given over to porn has fallen short of God's standard of holiness.

Notice that David did not try to minimize or justify his actions. Instead, he took ownership of every aspect of his moral failure. The phrases he used are possessive: *my* transgressions, *my* iniquity, *my* sin. He displayed a sincere heart of honesty with the Lord about what he did. While many would be tempted to shift the blame off themselves, David refused to do so. In fact, he never once mentioned Bathsheba in his prayer.

In light of his sinful condition, David prayed that God would do the work of blotting out, washing and cleansing him from his sin. The phrase *blot out* has the connotation of destroying from memory.[7] *Washing* and *cleansing* describe a deep, thorough process, much more involved than simply rinsing something off. This is not a quick "Sorry, Lord, forgive me" prayer, so he could move on with his life. He was asking the Lord to deeply cleanse every area of his heart so that the stain of his sin could be removed and forgotten. Spurgeon once wrote:

"The hypocrite is content if his garments are washed, but the true suppliant cries, 'wash me.' The careless soul is content with a nominal cleansing, but the truly awakened conscience desires a real and practical washing, and that of a most complete and efficient kind."[8]

131

True confession is not merely apologizing to the God while continuing in sin. That would lead to an endless cycle that never results in freedom. Instead, confession of sin means to come to the Lord with a sincere desire and *intention* to change.

REPENTANCE PRINCIPLE #3:

Make No Excuses

"For I acknowledge my transgressions, and my sin is always before me. Against You, You only, have I sinned, and done this evil in Your sight— That You may be found just when You speak, and blameless when You judge."

(vss. 3-4)

David acknowledged his sin to the Lord, keeping nothing in the dark. In doing so, he took full responsibility for his actions. He understood that Yahweh's role in the situation was Judge, and that he was guilty as charged in His courtroom. He did not approach the Judge prepared to enter a "not guilty" plea. He understood that his adulterous affair with Bathsheba had led him to break at least three of the Ten Commandments: coveting his neighbor's wife (#10), committing adultery (#7) and taking part in murder to cover it up (#6). What David did was no small infraction. Yet, he approached God in honesty and took responsibility for his sin.

The temptation that professing Christians experience when dealing with sin is to shift the blame onto other people or circumstances. They create a list of internal conclusions that alleviate their responsibility. This is exactly what I did when I was bound by pornography. I rationalized it until it seemed like a small flaw in my character. I blamed the fact that I had been exposed at a young age and pointed to some of the painful things I had experienced in life as reasons for my porn issue. In fact, I cut myself so much slack that I felt no urgency to get it out of my life, in spite of the fact that it continued for several years.

In contrast, David placed his fate in the hands of the Judge to decide his case. He refused to rationalize his sin; instead, he freely and fully confessed it. The man who wants to find true freedom must refuse the temptation to dodge responsibility. Only the man willing to own his sin will enjoy the blessing of repentance.

REPENTANCE PRINCIPLE #4:

Embrace the Truth

"Behold, I was brought forth in iniquity, and in sin my mother conceived me. Behold, You desire truth in the inward parts, and in the hidden part You will make me to know wisdom." (vss. 5-6)

David came to grips with his true spiritual condition as he walked through repentance. His thinking needed to change from pretending things were alright to coming into agreement with how the Lord saw his sinful heart. Notice that he did not try to highlight his great faith, his royal position or his history with Yahweh. Rather, he embraced his sinful state, admitting that sin was not just an action that he did, but a natural bent that was deeply interwoven into his being. Saying, "I was brought forth in iniquity" is a far cry from, "God, forgive me for that one thing I did wrong." David understood that his heart was wicked, and that adultery and murder were only symptoms of a much deeper problem. John Piper commented on this verse:

> "Some people use their inborn or inbred corruption to diminish their personal guilt. David does the opposite. For him the fact that he committed adultery and murdered and lied are expressions of something worse: He is by nature that way. If God does not rescue him, he will do more and more evil."[9]

Men in sin must also come to terms with the fact that their porn issue points to a deeper problem: their sinful hearts. If they continue to insist on believing that they are good Christian men with an isolated porn issue, it will prevent repentance from doing its powerful work in their hearts. Through repentance, the Lord wants to do much more than remove the symptoms of sexual sin; He wants to change your heart so that you live differently. Only by coming into agreement with His assessment of your condition will you experience lasting transformation.

David had to come to terms with his deception. We know he was hiding his sin for the period of Bathsheba's pregnancy because their baby was born before Nathan's confrontation. Like many of us, the king was a master at secrecy. Keeping his adultery under wraps was his top priority, even to the extent of coordinating the murder of one of his loyal soldiers. Now that his sin had been brought into the light, David realized that this is what God wanted all along: truth in his inward parts.

The Lord desires that our inner lives be permeated with truth. He wants us to be free from hypocrisy, with no skeletons hidden in our closets and no spiritual masks draped over our faces. Just like David, many reading these words have presented one image to others, while keeping a great deal hidden. They also continued with the motions of spirituality, making sure everyone thought of them as godly men. Through the process of repentance, they can allow God to overthrow the lies they have embraced and establish truth in their hearts.

REPENTANCE PRINCIPLE #5:

Cry Out to God

"Purge me with hyssop, and I shall be clean;
Wash me, and I shall be whiter than snow.
Make me hear joy and gladness,
that the bones You have broken may rejoice.
Hide Your face from my sins, and blot out all my iniquities." (vss. 7-9)

You can hear the desperation in David's heart as he pleaded with the Lord. He asked Yahweh to make him even whiter than snow on the inside. Anyone who has attempted to walk with God while remaining in sin understands what it feels like to wrestle with a dirty conscience. It is that nagging feeling that is always there below the surface, reminding you that something is off. You can try to distract yourself from a dirty conscience or pretend it is not there, but there is only one way to have it cleansed, and that is through repentance. David looked to God and said, "Please, remove the stain of my sin from my conscience. Make me clean again!"

He then asked God to make him hear *joy* and *gladness*. These words describe a deep, heartfelt exuberance that is more than merely a sense of relief or shallow happiness. The unrepentant man is devoid of this internal rejoicing because his sin prevents him from experiencing these blessings. But to those who cry out to the Lord from the depths of their heart, He will respond by replacing the anxiety, depression and guilt with His peace, joy and gladness.

One of my first assignments from my counselor at Pure Life Ministries was to practice the discipline of crying out to the Lord. I was told to do it even when I did not feel like it. What I discovered was, as I continually asked the Lord for help, even when it seemed to be a lifeless exercise, it caused me to place my attention on Him as my source of hope. Over time, that call for help began to take root in my heart. All these years later, it is still a daily practice that reminds me of my dependency on the Lord for everything.

I suppose all addicts have hoped for the "easy-button" fix. The thinking goes something like this: "If God will just touch me and take this thing out of my life, I could finally get free." Of course, that attitude requires no true brokenness, no pain on their part, no cleaning up the messes they have created, no confrontation and no strain on their relationships. Essentially, it would be freedom at no cost to themselves. I discovered on my own journey what David realized: there is no pain-free version of repentance. A man in bondage needs to cry out to the Lord to do whatever it takes in his heart to set him free.

REPENTANCE PRINCIPLE #6:

Focus on Your Relationship with God

"Create in me a clean heart, O God, and renew a steadfast spirit within me.
Do not cast me away from Your presence,
and do not take Your Holy Spirit from me.
Restore to me the joy of Your salvation,
and uphold me by Your generous Spirit." (vss. 10-12)

Some might suppose that getting free from porn requires an extreme focus on it. The belief is that if we can get our minds wrapped around the intricacies of why we cannot stop sinning, maybe we can "figure out" what is going on and fix it. However, doing that causes our minds to become fixated on ourselves rather than on the Source of our freedom. While David did acknowledge his sin, he turned his focus to his relationship with God. He did not rehash all the details to try to learn how to avoid it in the future. He was completely focused on restoring his relationship with the Lord and making sure there were no barriers between them.

David's requests reveal that he was primarily concerned about transformation. He asked God to create a clean heart inside of him, free from the sin that once controlled him. He also requested a steadfast spirit. That word *steadfast* comes from the root word that means "be set up, established, fixed" like a house on pillars.[10] The king realized that unless God did a brand-new work in his life, he would be apt to go back and commit the same sin again. He knew he needed a spiritual fortitude that could go the distance with the Lord.

David pleaded to be kept in fellowship with the Holy Spirit. Perhaps he was thinking of Saul, his predecessor, from whom the Spirit of the Lord departed.[11] He prayed, "Please don't let that happen to me. All I care about is your presence. Do whatever you want to me, but please don't leave me!" He was a desperate man crying out for more than just forgiveness; he desired God Himself.

In verse 12, David asked for the restoration of his joy in the Lord. I am certain he could remember his time as a young shepherd in the fields, tending to the sheep, singing to the Lord and enjoying His presence. It was before he achieved all his fame and fortune, when life was much less complicated. In this prayer, he looked back and said, "Lord, please give that back to me. Restore the joy of Your salvation!" He had tried to find joy in what this sinful world offers, but it was not able to satisfy. Now, he chose to look to the Lord to restore that sense of awe and wonder he once had.

Each of these requests reflect David's desire to restore his fellowship with God. How different is the man who is only trying to escape the painful consequences of sin. The prayer, "God, please set me free from porn," and "I'm desperate to be in right standing with you," reveal two very different motivations. Turn your focus on your relationship with God, and you will find that repentance will have a much deeper impact on your spiritual life than simply ending a sinful practice.

REPENTANCE PRINCIPLE #7:

Become a Broken Sacrifice

"For You do not desire sacrifice, or else I would give it;
You do not delight in burnt offering.
The sacrifices of God are a broken spirit, a broken and a contrite heart—
These, O God, You will not despise." (vss. 16-17)

In a consumer-based society, we tend to discard things when they break. Sometimes we will repair an object to restore its value or usefulness, but often we just throw it away. Landfills are evidence of how many items people toss in the trash on a regular basis. As humans, we typically see little value in things that are broken.

In contrast, David received a powerful revelation about Yahweh's positive attitude toward broken things. He recognized that God did not desire outward sacrifice without inward contrition. Although animal sacrifice was an important part of the worship routine in ancient Israel, David realized that the Lord was looking for something much deeper; He was looking for brokenness in His people. Rather than discarding broken people, the Lord seeks and restores them.

The brokenness that the Lord wants for us is not the kind that makes us useless. Nor is it punitive in nature. It is a different type of brokenness that aligns our stubborn, sinful wills to His. While godly brokenness involves pain, it is a necessary element to finding freedom from sin. This is why David explained that God does not despise "a broken and contrite heart." Again from Spurgeon:

"A heart crushed is a fragrant heart. Men despise those who are contemptible in their own eyes, but the Lord sees not as man sees. He despises what men esteem, and values that which they despise.

137

Never yet has God spurned a lowly, weeping penitent, and never will he while God is love, and while Jesus is called the man who receives sinners."[12]

Before his repentance, David had been very confident in his own abilities when it came to dealing with sin. He had attempted to fix everything in his own wisdom and strength. His heart was hardened and his will was unbroken. However, he finally came to the end of his rope and laid it all down at the feet of the Lord as a living sacrifice unto Him. His willingness to become a broken sacrifice put him in the right position to receive God's mercy.

The Apostle Paul gave us insight regarding godly contrition in his second letter to the Corinthian church. He explained that *godly sorrow* produces repentance which leads to salvation.[13] However, he refers to another type of sorrow as well, called *worldly sorrow*. This is the emotion most people feel when they get caught doing something wrong. Worldly sorrow is extremely deceptive because it feels like legitimate remorse, but it will not bring about change in our lives because it does not produce brokenness in our hearts. In fact, Paul tells us that it leads to death.[14]

It is clear in Psalm 51 that David experienced godly sorrow because he was concerned about more than how his circumstances had negatively impacted his life. His focus was on his relationship with God and making sure he was in right standing before Him. We too should ask the Lord to give us godly sorrow that leads to heart transformation. We must be willing to become broken and contrite. If we do, we can become a sacrifice that is acceptable and pleasing to God.

REPENTANCE PRINCIPLE #8:

Bear the Fruit

"Then I will teach transgressors Your ways,
and sinners shall be converted to You.
Deliver me from the guilt of bloodshed, O God, the God of my salvation,
and my tongue shall sing aloud of Your righteousness.

O Lord, open my lips, and my mouth shall show forth Your praise.
Do good in Your good pleasure to Zion; Build the walls of Jerusalem.
Then You shall be pleased with the sacrifices of righteousness,
with burnt offering and whole burnt offering;
Then they shall offer bulls on Your altar." (vss. 13-15, 18-19)

In these verses, David makes several statements that reflect on life after repentance. When a man is looking at what seems to be an unscalable mountain in front of him, his perspective is often skewed. It can be difficult to imagine what life would look like in freedom when all he has known is fruitless effort and defeat. However, David was able to look beyond his immediate need for forgiveness and see what would happen as a result of his repentance process.

For example, he mentioned that his repentance would lead to sinners being converted to God (vs. 13) and that he would freely worship the Lord and praise His name. (vs. 14) Also, pleasing sacrifices would be offered to the Lord. (vs. 19) Each of these is an aspect of fruit that David understood would come as he became the godly man and righteous king that God desired.

The lifestyle of a truly repentant man will provide evidence that he has changed in a tangible way. I have seen a lot of repentance in my years of ministry: both genuine and insincere. Nothing excites me more than to see a man who truly repents of his sin, receives forgiveness and restoration from the Lord, and goes on to live his life in freedom. On the other hand, there is nothing more heartbreaking than to witness a man who seems to have a genuine desire to repent, and makes some strides to change, only to end up back in the spiritual wastelands. Often, he ends up in worse shape than before his supposed "repentance." My experience used to be much more like the latter description.

I went to a Bible college that invited people to the altar if they wanted to respond to the Lord in a tangible way during chapel services. My solution to my porn addiction was to respond to every altar call that was given and cry out to the Lord. The problem was that I was not prepared to do what was required to rid myself of my idol. I thought I was sincere, but the fact that I continued in sin proved otherwise. There were plenty of practical steps that I could have taken to eliminate the sin, but I refused. I needed to realize that true biblical repentance always results in tangible fruit.

In Luke 3:8, John the Baptist commanded the people to "produce fruit in keeping with repentance."(NIV) If you ask the question, "How do I know if I have repented of pornography," the answer is that you should be able to find evidence of that repentance in your life. If you are wondering whether a trip you took to the altar was true repentance or merely lip-service, just look for the proof of it. If we really mean business with God, we will do whatever it takes to be right with Him. People who have wet eyes on Sunday—but no change on Monday—need to examine the sincerity of their repentance.

True repentance should cause a desire to rid your life of sin. Porn should not be something you can run right back to without a second thought. Although temptation may still come, there should be a godly fear that prevents you from giving in, and a fervent desire to remain in good standing with the Lord. Charles Finney once said it this way: "Repentance is a change of mind toward God and sin. It is not only a change of views, but a change of the ultimate preference or choice of the soul and of action."[15] Deleting porn from our lives will result in a severing of our relationship with it. David's story shows us what it looks like to truly bear the fruit of the repentance process.

THE INVITATION INTO FREEDOM

What about you? Are you still trying to figure out this sexual sin issue through your own wisdom and ideas? Have you finally come to the end of yourself? Have you experienced the contrition that David talked about? If you are allowing the biblical truths in this chapter to do what they are intended to do, brokenness should be forming inside of you.

My encouragement to you as we conclude this chapter is this: "Don't resist the breaking down process." It was this process that transformed my life in 2011. I needed the Lord to reveal my heart and expose my sinful attitudes. I needed to experience the sense of being trapped under the weight of my sin with no way out. That breaking down process is the very thing that drove me to the cross. David's psalm shows that God does not discard broken things. Isaiah 42:3 says, "A bruised reed He will not break, and smoking flax He will not quench." What an amazing aspect of God's nature!

The man who is involved with pornography needs to come to the place of full surrender. Many cry out for freedom, but do not want to be broken. They resist the very process God uses to set a man free because it is often uncomfortable and inconvenient. Our insistence on having comfort and convenience is what got us into sexual sin in the first place. Instead, the Lord will bring us through repentance in a way that costs us everything and transforms our lives both externally and internally.

You might say, "But I *am* desperate. I'm at the end of my rope." Okay, but are you desperate to be in right relationship with God? Or are you simply hoping to get out of the mess you created? Are you willing to put this book down right now, get on your face and call out to the Lord for freedom? It might not seem like much, but it will put your heart in a perfect posture to receive from Him. Our Heavenly Father will not turn away from a true prayer from the heart.

If David's prayer from Psalm 51 does not describe your internal world, do not be discouraged. 2 Timothy 2:25 says that repentance is a gift that God grants. He wants these qualities to be true in your heart, and it starts with a conversation with Him. Consider praying something like this:

"God, I see how desperate David was, and how sincerely he threw himself at your mercy. If I'm honest, I'm not there, but I want to be. If this is the pathway to freedom, please grant me repentance like David experienced. Put a cry in my heart for You like I've never had before. Bring me to the end of myself and allow me to experience brokenness in my heart. In Jesus' Name, Amen."

CHANGE OF HEART REQUIRED

The stories of David and Solomon have many interesting parallels. Both men were selected by God to lead the nation of Israel as kings, and both had a love for the Lord. Each of these men also had a propensity toward sexual sin. However, they ended up in very different places.

The contrast between the way that David and Solomon responded to the Lord about the sexual sin in their lives is instructive for the man who wants to get free from pornography. David's contrite heart led to transformation in his life. It did not remove the consequences of his sin, but the process of repentance allowed David to walk in freedom from it. By contrast, Solomon refused to walk through the repentance process and therefore remained in bondage.

Just like Solomon, a man addicted to pornography does not get into that position overnight. He did not just wake up one day completely pure and go to bed that night given over to sexual sin. Yet, so many of us expect to read a book, listen to a sermon, or go to a conference and have it all disappear instantaneously. As we move into the next part of the book, my challenge for every man is to ask himself the questions, "Am I ready to walk through the painful, messy, beautiful and liberating process of repentance that David went through? Am I willing to do what it takes to get free?" Your answer to those questions will determine the effectiveness of this process of deleting porn from your life.

In the following chapter, we will examine the next step of the freedom journey. I would encourage you to pray right now that the Lord will open your heart to the process of repentance that is about to become very practical.

CHAPTER 8

Return:// freedom-begins-here

PRAYER POINTS

- Pray that God will reveal specific areas of your heart where breakthrough is needed

- Pray that the Lord will bless your life with a spirit of brokenness that will lead to sincere repentance over your sin

- Pray that God will help develop a cry in your heart for Him that will teach you how to depend on Him daily

DISCUSSION QUESTIONS

1. Find other passages in the Bible that speak about God's mercy and compassion. What do they say about the Lord's character that is encouraging to the man in need?

2. What are the typical excuses and rationalizations that professing Christians in sexual sin make about their lifestyle?

3. Do you think that men typically embrace or resist the process of being broken by the Lord? Why do you think that is?

4. What spiritual fruit does a man in sexual sin forfeit? How does repentance pave the way for that fruit to grow in a man's life?

5. What stands out to you about the process of repentance highlighted in this chapter that you did not understand before reading it?

PERSONAL APPLICATION QUESTIONS

1. Which of the eight principles of repentance listed in this chapter stands out to you the most as needed in your own life?

2. Before reading this chapter, would you have considered yourself a repentant person? Has that changed after studying Psalm 51?

3. Considering the process of repentance being laid out in this chapter, what practical steps can you take to embrace repentance and walk it out?

PART THREE://

the-immediate-solution

9

Increase Brightness://

come-into-the-light

WHEN A MAN ASKS ME FOR PRACTICAL advice on getting free from porn, this is truly where the "rubber meets the road." While most do not want to consider this principle, the repentance process *requires* bringing our sin into the light. I learned this lesson the hard way. For years, I had attempted to overcome my sin in secret. I believed that the Lord would set me free without anyone finding out so that I could avoid the pain that was sure to follow if I exposed my sin. I convinced myself that it was better that I confess to God alone to spare the pain of my loved ones. The pressure to confess was often overwhelming at times. I remember thinking, "If I just come out in the open with everything, maybe I can finally get free from this nightmare." Yet, my list of reasons to avoid exposure kept me locked in a prison of secrecy.

These excuses were not completely unfounded. My eventual confession did indeed put my marriage, ministry and reputation in jeopardy. I was aware that I would face painful consequences if my sin came out, but the longer I kept it covered, the higher the stakes became. Bringing my sin into the light early on would have saved myself and those I thought I was "protecting" a greater degree of pain and humiliation. I realize now that it was my stubborn pride that actually kept me in bondage.

During that season in my life, I held onto a fantasy that in our later years my wife and I would be sitting in rocking chairs on our front porch, and we would have the following conversation:

"Do you remember when we were younger, and I told you I was struggling with pornography in Bible college?" I would tell her.

"Yes, that was so many years ago, but I remember it. When we were dating, right?"

"Well, yes. That was what I had told you. And I tried to make you and everyone else think that I was completely free. But in reality, it was a couple of years into our marriage before God really set me free. It's been over fifty years since I've sinned in that area."

My elderly wife of several decades would look at me with love in her eyes and say, "Well, dear. That was so long ago. Thanks for telling me, but it's no big deal. I'm glad that God helped you out with that. But it's over and done with now."

This was merely an attempt to justify my silence because I was too much of a coward to face the consequences of the choices I was making. It was pure fantasy to think that I was going to escape this powerful addiction with no pain or repercussions. The fatal flaw with that plan was that repentance *was never going to happen until I confessed to my wife.* It was not going to simply resolve itself. My unwillingness to confess was making repentance an *impossibility.* Had I understood that truth, perhaps it would have been enough to cause me to take that nagging internal voice more seriously.

Many men share the same flawed thinking. They convince themselves that God is going to miraculously set them free without the mess and pain of an open confession. It is a plan that may be convenient and comfortable, but it is also delusional. The self-centered thinking that undergirds a life of sexual sin is the same that insists on secrecy. Trying to convince themselves that everything will work itself out eventually is just a coward's way of avoiding responsibility for their sin.

Let me state it plainly: There is no way for you to get free other than complete honesty. I absolutely believe that the Lord is a supernatural God who is able to set men free. If you are still bound up in sin, it is not because He is lacking the power and ability to set you free. It is because you have been demanding that He do it outside of His normal way of operating. In short, there is no freedom without transparency.

Let me ask you this: If you were able to get free without telling anyone else, why are you still in bondage today? It is time to do something more radical so that freedom can become a reality in your life.

HIDDEN IN THE TENT

The life of Achan from Joshua 7 provides an illustration of many men sitting in our churches. His story takes place during the Israelite's conquest of the Promised Land. After an impressive battle against Jericho, in which God supernaturally tore the walls of the city down, Joshua sent men to spy out the nearby city of Ai. They returned with the recommendation that Joshua send a limited number of troops because the city was small and unable to defend itself against Israel. However, that proved to be a failing plan as the Israelites experienced a humiliating defeat.

After praying to the Lord, it was revealed to Joshua that the reason Israel had been routed by their enemies was because someone had taken forbidden plunder from Jericho. Yahweh instructed Joshua to call a mandatory assembly the following morning for the entire nation. In that meeting, He would reveal the identity of the man who had committed the sin. In the short time between the announcement and the actual gathering of the people, Achan had an opportunity to confess what he had done. We cannot know what kind of mercy might have been shown to him if he had, but at least he could have ended his story with some dignity as a man willing to own up for his sin.

Instead, the evening passed, the morning came, and Achan said nothing. Joshua went through the painstaking process of whittling down the massive group of people first by tribe…then clan…then family…and then household. Still, Achan stood mute as the crowd grew smaller and smaller. He dug in his heels and waited until God had to identify him specifically. The camp then proceeded to stone him, his family, and even his animals to rid the camp of sin according to God's command.

I have met men in the church who have been just like Achan. Some were leaders of ministries and perceived to be men of God yet lived in secret sin. Like Achan, they had a window of opportunity to bring their darkness into the light. Yet, because of their refusal, the Lord orchestrated circumstances to expose their secret lives. While some might consider God unmerciful for allowing a man's sin to be publicly exposed, the truth is that it is pure *mercy* for the Lord to shine His light on secret sin. What if the Lord allowed the man to continue in sin? How much deeper might he go? How many more lives would be destroyed? However, having his sin come out that way is far riskier than making the decision to come clean of his own volition. It simply does not look good when a man is exposed by circumstances rather than confession, because it gives everyone around him the impression, "He wasn't planning on telling anybody and the only reason he is honest now is because he was forced by his circumstances."

The deception of keeping our sin in the darkness is that it gives the false impression that it is truly hidden. But Jeremiah 16:17 contradicts this fallacy: "For My eyes are on all their ways; they are not hidden from My face, nor is their iniquity hidden from My eyes." Yahweh was fully aware of every action Achan took. So, there was never any possibility that he was going to avoid facing his sin head-on. Procrastinating did nothing to change the outcome. As is the case with any professing Christian who hides his sin, it only deepens the guilt. As Steve Gallagher points out:

> "It is not enough for a person to come to grips with his sin. He must come into the light with others. Darkness is the devil's domain. Those who refuse to come into the light about their sin are choosing to remain in darkness."[1]

When I hear an unfortunate report about a minister being exposed for sexual sin, it makes me wonder how many times he had refused the Lord's prompting to come into the light. How often did he justify keeping his sin in the dark rather than taking the opportunities he was given to tell his spouse or superiors? How much pain could he have avoided had he come clean at the beginning of his compromise? At any point in time, he could have chosen to walk in the light rather than keeping it out of the public eye. God is providing you an opportunity to avoid the cowardice of Achan by choosing to walk in the light right now.

PRINCIPLES FOR HEALTHY CONFESSION

Assuming you are convinced that confession is the next step in your repentance process, you probably have many questions about what that might look like on a practical level. Allow me to provide three principles that will help make that confession healthy and effective.

PRINCIPLE #1:
Choose Who You Will Tell

Based on what I have already shared, I do not think the question should ever be, "Do I need to confess my sin to somebody?" The only questions are, "Who will I tell?" and "When will I tell them?" Exposure does not mean that we need to broadcast our sin to everyone around us. Depending on the depth of the sin and our position of influence, the number of people that need to be involved will vary. At minimum, sexual sin must be confessed to a spouse; that is non-negotiable. I have never encountered a situation where I did not think this was the right course of action. This is because pornography is a sin between a husband and wife. I exhort married men, "Not telling your wife doesn't make it go away." She needs to know, and that conversation needs to happen as soon as possible.

There is nothing wrong with first confessing to a spiritual leader—whether you are married or single. That person can then walk you through the process alongside your spouse, or parents if you are a minor. If you are a minister, you need to bring this to light with a leader who is above

153

you in rank or a brother in the Lord whom you trust. This person needs to be a godly man with spiritual maturity, like a pastor, minister or strong Christian friend. It must also be someone who will love you enough to make sure you follow through on your pursuit of freedom.

The point is that you find *someone*. Do the hard thing and bring it into the light. Might there be some difficult repercussions? Of course. But living in secret sin is not a better alternative. Carrying the secret to your grave is not the answer. The longer you keep up the charade, the more painful confession will be. As the saying goes, "There is no time like the present."

PRINCIPLE #2:
Avoid Partial Confession

You must resist the temptation to give a partial confession. As men, our tendency when confessing sin is often to crack open the door of our lives just enough so that people can get a glimpse inside but not actually divulge everything. Men have a propensity to confess a little bit at first, and then uncover layers of information progressively when they feel pressed or unable to take the guilt of keeping it hidden. If you are confessing this way to your wife, it is like pulling off a Band-Aid and reopening the wound every time. I encourage men to confess everything immediately, keeping nothing hidden.

Of course, this does not mean that you must share every graphic detail of your sin. You must also use a great deal of wisdom in dealing with your wife. Before entering this conversation, I strongly suggest you bathe it in prayer. Pick a time when the two of you can sit down together without interruption. Tell her that you need to share something important with her. The following are some examples of what you could say:

- *"I have been viewing pornography for our entire married life."*

- *"I had an affair with a girl from work that lasted two months."*

- *"I have been hooking up with prostitutes for years and it only stopped for a short time when we got married."*

Those statements tell the whole truth without being overly explicit. Then brace yourself to face her anger. You have deeply hurt her, and it is your responsibility to let her vent her pain without retaliation. Determine in yourself that you are going to accept whatever comes as humbly as possible. You owe her that.

When it comes to the person you are exposing your sin to, it is important that he knows exactly what he is dealing with. If it is a pastor or biblical counselor, you need to be transparent. I fully understand the feeling of shame and embarrassment that comes from saying out loud what you have done in private. I know from experience the desire to minimize your sin, but if you hope to come into real victory, you must come clean with all of it. For instance, if it involves violence or underage people, your spiritual leader needs to know that sort of detail. If you have been spending a thousand dollars a month on porn, do not pretend that it was only a hundred. You get the point.

Trust me, whether you are confessing to a wife, a parent or a pastor, be real, be honest, and get it all out right at the beginning. You will find that it is much less painful in the long-term than having to keep having conversations like, "Well, I know I told you this was all that happened, but I wasn't being entirely truthful. The reality is…"

PRINCIPLE #3:

Do Not Delay

There are some men reading these words who are having an intense spiritual battle inside. I can only imagine what would have been going through my mind if I was confronted this way when I was hiding my sin. The Lord will knock on the door of our hearts trying to get us to deal with the sin in our lives. If we refuse Him, our hearts will harden little by little. Every time we shove that conviction down and continue in sin, it is like another layer of callous being added. Eventually, His voice will be nothing more than a whisper as we train ourselves to shut His conviction out of our consciences. The most frightening possibility is becoming so hardhearted that the Holy Spirit stops knocking and gives us over to our sin.[2]

It is by no accident that you are reading these words. The Holy Spirit has orchestrated this in your life because He is calling out to you in His mercy. He wants to set you free and keep you free, but *you* must make the decision to respond. If you have not confessed your sin, set this book down right now. Make the phone call. Send the text or email. Initiate the process of exposure. Do something to take a step in that direction.

What too many men do is procrastinate when they feel the conviction of the Holy Spirit. They say, "It's really not a good time right now. My pastor is probably busy. I can't imagine how my wife will respond. I'm going to do it, just not today." And because this has been the pattern of their lives since they first started hiding, they know how to deceive themselves to believe that their intentions are enough to appease their guilty conscience. It feels good to pretend that they will make the right choice down the road. However, as Bernard of Clairvaux once wrote, "Hell is full of good wishes and desires."[3]

Each man reading this needs to become painfully honest with himself about what he really wants. You know that prolonging the process will just lead to more pain, deeper addiction, more depraved content and possibly adultery, fornication, or any other outward act that you will regret for the rest of your life. There is no better day than today. Sure, all of us wish we could go back to some prior date and expose everything in a less painful way. Unfortunately, going back in time is impossible, so we must take action now. The Bible declares, "Now is the day of salvation"[4] and "Today, if you will hear His voice, do not harden your hearts."[5] This is a threshold that must be crossed on the pathway to freedom.

YOUR CHANCE TO DO THE RIGHT THING

Think about men in Scripture who might have had a different story if they had been willing to walk in the light about their internal lives. What if Adam had a conversation with God before taking the fruit offered by

Eve? What if Cain had been willing to talk to his parents about the anger burning inside of him before heading out to the field to find Abel? What if David had shared his lustful tendencies with Nathan before he called for Bathsheba? What if Judas had been honest with the other disciples about his intentions to betray Jesus? The list could go on and on.

I wasted years of my life because I was unwilling to confess my sin in the beginning. I could have avoided exposing myself to a lot of perversion. I know that the Lord has done a great work of redemption and that He is a redeemer of the time. But I also know that my sin had a huge price tag attached to it, and that it nearly cost me my marriage, my family and my ministry. While we cannot rewind the clock to a better time to confess, I pray that sharing my personal regrets will convince you to do what you need to do *now*.

The next chapter will provide another practical step that must be taken in the repentance process which involves making sure the doors to pornography are tightly shut.

CHAPTER 9

Increase Brightness://

come-into-the-light

PRAYER POINTS

- Pray that all areas of hidden sin and deception will be revealed in your life and that God will give you the courage to confess them to someone close to you

- Pray for other men who will read this chapter and experience a significant spiritual battle in putting it into practice

- Pray that the Lord will show incredible mercy to married men who will confess to their wives as they walk through this process

DISCUSSION QUESTIONS

1. Have you witnessed the painful experience of a man getting exposed for secret sin in his life? What happened as a result of that situation? Might it have been different if he had come clean on his own?

2. Why do you think that Achan did not come clean the night before the assembly when he understood what was going to happen the following morning?

3. Do you think it is possible for a man to get free from pornography without any involvement with other people in his life? If so, how might the probability increase if he includes others in his pursuit of freedom?

4. What are some of the important qualities this chapter brings out that someone you are confessing to should have? Can you think of other qualities?

5. This chapter exhorts men, "You know that prolonging the process will just lead to more pain, deeper addiction, more depraved content and possibly adultery, fornication, or any other outward act that you will regret for the rest of your life." With that in mind, can you think of any valid reasons for a man to keep his sin secret?

PERSONAL APPLICATION QUESTIONS

1. For Achan, it was a Babylonian garment and some gold and silver that caused him to disobey the Lord. Other than pornography, what are the idols in your life that you have been willing to disobey the Lord to keep?

2. What conversations are you most afraid to have? What fears are keeping you from sharing your secret sin with others in your life?

3. Who is the first person that you need to come to the light with? When will you have that conversation?

10

Cut:// close-every-door

EVERY MAN ADDICTED TO PORN HAS opened a door to the enemy in his life. He may have made half-hearted attempts to avoid temptation and even had temporary bouts of abstinence, but eventually the enemy's offer was too enticing to resist. Most reading these words can relate to the endless cycle of vowing to quit porn, trying to stay pure, then falling back into it again. This pattern needs to change if a man is going to learn how to walk in true freedom. To do this, every door to temptation must be tightly shut. If a man leaves a door even slightly cracked, the enemy will use that access point to continually lure him back into his sin. Prolonged freedom will never happen if the door is left ajar. Before we examine specific ways to make sure that the doors to temptation are kept closed, let us first consider a passage of Scripture aimed at warning men about the danger of sexual temptation.

THE PROVERBS 7 SCENARIO

Solomon's seventh proverb illustrates what can happen when a man foolishly leaves a door open to temptation. The two characters in the story are a foolish young man (vs 7); and an immoral woman "with the attire of a harlot, and a crafty heart." (vs. 10) The young man is walking through town and takes a pathway that runs alongside her house "in the twilight, in the evening." (vs. 9) Even if you have not read this story before, it is easy to guess where it is going. It has all the elements of a trashy porn script.

The immoral woman is a perfect personification of sexual temptation. We are told about her: "She was loud and rebellious, her feet would not stay at home. At times she was outside, at times in the open square, lurking at every corner." (vss. 11-12) Just like temptation, this promiscuous woman was on the prowl. She was not sitting at home, waiting for a man to knock on her door. Rather, she was actively seeking her next victim.

Just like the young man in this story, we also have an enemy who seeks to lure us into temptation. 1 Peter 5:8 implores us, "Be sober, be vigilant; because your adversary the devil walks about like a roaring lion, seeking whom he may devour." Similar to the woman in the story, Satan is actively seeking men to lure into sexual sin. We must develop a spiritual alertness if we are going to avoid the fate of the young man in Proverbs 7.

The woman's interaction with the young man is very revealing. Her strategies mirror those of the devil when tempting Christian men. First, she declares that she had fulfilled her spiritual duties for the day by offering sacrifices to God. (vs. 14) Her first words to the young man are not an invitation to indulge in sin but a spiritual rationalization. It is the same tactic the enemy uses when tempting men into porn. He tells them, "You're a good Christian man. You went to church this week. You pray and read the Bible. A little compromise isn't such a big deal. What's it going to hurt to crack the door open a little bit?"

Second, she appeals to his flesh by describing the perfumes that she used to prepare her bed for him, shamelessly saying, "Come, let us take our fill of love until morning; Let us delight ourselves with love." (vss. 16-18) The seductress is trying to get the young man to focus on the immediate pleasure he can experience, rather than the long-term consequences. What an apt illustration of sexual temptation! When a man is tempted to look at porn, the longer he entertains those thoughts, the more his mind can only focus on the initial pleasure he will experience. The devil never tells us the end of the story. His strategy is to get us to keep the door to temptation open long enough that we reach the point of no return. The only way to prevent that downward spiral is to refuse to open a door to temptation in the first place.

Third, the woman assuages the young man's fear of getting caught by reassuring him that her husband is away. (vss. 19-20) Think about what she is saying to him: "You can indulge in sexual sin, and no one ever has to find out." These are the same words the enemy will whisper into the ear of a man he is trying to tempt into sin. If he believed that other people would find out about his sin, he would probably close the door to temptation. However, the promise of secrecy is often an effective strategy to get a man to open the door.

At each stage of the conversation, the young man in Proverbs 7 lingers. He could have closed the door at any point, but he allowed her strategy to lure him into sin. Solomon tells us the following about this young man's fate:

> With her enticing speech she caused him to yield, with her flattering lips she seduced him. Immediately he went after her, as an ox goes to the slaughter, or as a fool to the correction of the stocks, till an arrow struck his liver. As a bird hastens to the snare, he did not know it would cost his life... **(vss. 21-23)**

The Bible is trying to help us understand the danger of opening the door to sexual temptation. The man who walks through life like the young man in Solomon's story is setting himself up for devastating failure. Any door left open to sexual temptation is an invitation to the devil to keep us in bondage. We are no match for the enemy in our own strength or determination. He has been successfully tempting men into sexual sin for thousands of years. If we exercise biblical wisdom by taking the proper steps to navigate the battlefield of temptation, then we are told that we may be kept "from the immoral woman, from the seductress who flatters with her words." (vs. 5) A modern translation might say, "If you obey the truths of God's Word, they can help you close the door to the temptation to look at porn and insulate you from the enemy's strategies." In order to avoid falling into the Proverbs 7 trap, a man must develop the skill of resisting temptation rather than succumbing to it. He must learn to properly close the doors to temptation that he has allowed to remain open.

RADICAL AMPUTATION REQUIRED

Jesus provides a powerful principle that relates to a man's battle against sexual sin in the Sermon on the Mount:

> "You have heard that it was said to those of old, 'You shall not commit adultery.' But I say to you that whoever looks at a woman to lust for her has already committed adultery with her in his heart. If your right eye causes you to sin, pluck it out and cast it from you; for it is more profitable for you that one of your members perish, than for your whole body to be cast into hell. And if your right hand causes you to sin, cut it off and cast it from you; for it is more profitable for you that one of your members perish, than for your whole body to be cast into hell." (Matthew 5:27-30)

In the context of sexual sin, Jesus makes a very clear call to what some refer to as *radical amputation*. His main point is that it would be better to live without something useful in our lives if it causes us to sin. Jesus' attitude when it comes to dealing with sexual sin may seem extreme. He is suggesting that we make radical changes for the sake of purity. His philosophy is, "Temporary loss is always worth eternal gain." I do not think anyone would argue with Him about His logic. Certainly, if sin can drag us into hell, we ought to address it with fierce intensity. If anything is standing in the way of our relationship with God, it needs to be dealt with severely and immediately if we are going to find true and lasting freedom. We need to be willing to sacrifice in our fight against temptation if that is what is required.

What does that process look like on a practical basis? Closing doors to temptation involves insulating ourselves from all access to pornography. It can help to answer the question, "If I was really determined to look at porn today, where could I find it?" That tells you the location of the doors that need to be closed. While this could entail possessing a stash of printed pornography somewhere that needs to be destroyed, my assumption is that most readers are accessing porn on a digital device. In fact, Barna reports that, "Pornography has gone almost completely digital."[1]

The following are some options to quickly close the door to porn in order to continue on the journey to freedom.***

Software:

I am very grateful for the many companies who have stepped up in recent years to provide software to address the issues of immorality on the internet. There are two primary functions that software offers. The first is an accountability system, which keeps track of the searches and websites visited on a device and then sends reports to a designated accountability partner. The report will highlight any inappropriate content that might have been detected. Accountability software brings other people into the situation, which provides a level of *awareness* about what a man is doing online.

The second function is filtering software. This is designed to block pornographic content so that it is not even accessible. The settings can be tweaked to control which categories of websites are allowed and you can add blacklisted websites as needed. This provides a level of *prevention* from exposure to porn. My personal preference is to use both accountability and filtering software to provide maximum protection.

There are several companies that create and maintain these types of software. How each works and how effective it will be varies depending on several factors, including the type of device and operating system being used. It is worth noting that there is no flawless product that works 100% of the time. However, for the man who wants to be kept accountable, these

---

***Specific examples of available resources can be found in Appendix A.

types of software are a huge benefit. Knowing that your internet usage is being monitored by another person is an effective way to insulate yourself from temptation.

Most internet-connected devices offered in the market these days also contain some form of parental controls within its operating system. This is true of phones, video game systems, televisions and streaming services. While these controls can be useful if configured correctly, it should be noted that they are not designed to help men stay pure and that the values of the companies who create these controls are most likely different from the moral guidelines of Scripture. This is why using additional software from companies with biblical values is best.

Hardware:

Another way to tackle the issue of access is through the hardware itself. There are companies that offer customized Wi-Fi routers that are designed to block porn at the source, even before it reaches the devices connected to it. If the controls for the router are set up properly, this can provide some peace of mind that the connected devices are unable to access most pornographic materials. Just keep in mind that this does nothing to prevent porn on a phone that has its own data plan, as it can be disconnected from the Wi-Fi router and dodge any of its filtering capabilities.

There are also companies that have developed porn-free phones, which take the guesswork out of the equation by having a design that makes pornography impossible to access. It completely removes the temptation element, because the door to pornography does not exist. These devices are limited as to which apps come installed on them, which can be a downside for some. Each company has its own way of designing their phones, so the pros and cons of each model should be considered. However, if this is what it takes to delete porn from your life, it is completely worth the inconvenience factor. The principle for all technology is: *If you cannot properly filter it, get rid of it!*

Internet Based Technology:

When it comes to any technology that connects to the internet, the best posture is to always assume that none of it is safe from sexual temptation. There is a Proverbs 7 woman lurking within every online platform. That is because the pornography industry is going to make sure to capitalize on anything it can to make money. Because of the way new technology is impacting the daily life of most of our society, it is important that we address three types of technology specifically.

First, the world of social media is filled with traps and temptations that pop up even when you are not looking for them. Navigating it can be very challenging, and for most men who desire purity in their lives, completely avoiding social media will be the best option. Many Christian men have shared with me that social media is one of the biggest stumbling blocks to their purity. I have to ask them: "Is it worth having in your life if it causes you to stumble? Is it really something that you cannot live without?"

Second, artificial intelligence is another industry that is rapidly growing in popularity. However, it is filled with so much temptation that it is wise to avoid it completely. As one article states, "AI-generated pornography has quickly become one of the biggest and most troubling applications of the type of generative AI technology OpenAI has pioneered."[2] One of the unique challenges that AI presents is that its content is generative, and therefore the ability to filter it is nearly impossible. Christian companies will continue to do what they can to provide resources to keep men safe and accountable in this arena. However, the safest bet is simply to keep the door to those temptations closed.

Third, virtual reality is a developing technology that is another minefield of sexual temptation. As one source boasts, "The integration of VR into the adult entertainment industry is nothing short of revolutionary. It ushers in a new era of immersive experiences, where users can step into a virtual world of their desires."[3] Major porn companies like *Playboy* are finding creative ways to draw users into their own space in the metaverse.[4] The ability to connect with people sexually in an environment where you can remain anonymous makes the world of VR one that any man who desires purity must avoid.

Social media, artificial intelligence and virtual reality are examples of how the porn industry is using technology to its maximum potential to draw the hearts of men into their web of sexual sin. As one source reports, "The porn industry is often at the forefront of emerging technologies."[5] Because of this, closing these doors is an important part of the process of insulating yourself from temptation.

Outside Experts:

Some of the guidelines already provided will be a challenge for two types of men. First, there are those who are technologically challenged and will have an extremely difficult time setting up any kind of protection on their devices. Just the mention of software and hardware might have already flustered them. Others have the opposite problem. Because they are so technologically advanced, they can easily find loopholes in systems that are put in place. These are typically specialists in technological fields, and their concerns are valid. For both of those types of men, I would recommend getting outside help.

Some technology today can be so complex it is helpful to have a professional who understands the ins and outs of devices and internet connections to provide the best solutions. There are companies who have tackled this problem by providing personalized services to help men create a system that is difficult to circumvent and can provide ongoing support at keeping that system operating efficiently. A recommendation for a company that does this kind of work can be found in Appendix A.

HOW DESPERATE ARE YOU?

The sooner you close every door to porn, the faster you can deal with the underlying heart issues of sexual sin. Simply being porn-free is not God's primary goal; He wants to completely transform your heart. Continued access to porn will only circumvent that process. Based on what Jesus taught about radical amputation, what does it look like to cut off all access to porn in your life? I understand the answer to that question has implications. Some might involve minor yet inconvenient lifestyle changes. For others, it could call into question their ability to continue in their career. Each situation varies regarding how extreme the changes will need to be. Whatever the case may be, it is good to remember that our souls are more important than any temporal challenges we might face in our battle against sin.

I have had many conversations about closing doors with men who want to delete porn from their lives. They typically start like this:

"So, you are in bondage to pornography. How are you accessing porn?"

"It's mostly on my phone. Sometimes I view it on my laptop."

I typically would respond, "The first thing you need to do is cut off your internet access or find a way to eliminate all access to porn. Let's talk about how to set up a system that is going to ensure that you cannot find porn when you are tempted." The reaction that I get from the man in front of me tells me just about everything I need to know about how to approach him from that point on.

My experience with professing Christians who claim to want freedom can be divided into two distinct groups. Both groups seem to be in a similar place. Both are bound by pornography, and both claim they want to get free. Perhaps their sin was exposed, or maybe they confessed what they were doing because the pain of staying in it was too great to bear. Either way, they both seem to be desperate for freedom. The difference between these two groups becomes evident once I begin sharing what they need to do to find freedom.

First, let us consider the man who is broken and desperate for change. He will be determined to do whatever it takes to implement my advice. It is like a light bulb goes off as he realizes the benefit of simply closing the doors to temptation. He understands the implications for his marriage, kids and career if he does not get free. Even more importantly, he knows the fearful state of his soul and realizes that he cannot have a true relationship with God while remaining in sin. He may have legitimate concerns, such as the necessity of using his smartphone for work purposes, or the need to have internet access for school. But because he wants to please God, he is willing to have a conversation about it. It is never difficult to help this type of man. The hard work of plowing through a heart hardened by sin and selfishness is already underway. I have a lot of hope for guys in that condition. All they need is some godly counsel, lifestyle changes and accountability in their lives to walk in freedom.

Then there are those who immediately put up a defensive wall about their sin issues. They may act as though they want freedom, but their unwillingness to shut open doors to sin shows their insincerity. Not only are they unwilling to do whatever it takes to overcome, but the truth is they still love their sin and have no intention of giving it up. My message to this man is, "Come back when you are serious about getting free." I fear for him if the Lord does not find a way to wake him up to his fearful spiritual condition.

If you truly want to be free from porn, you must be all-in. I have never seen a man who is on the fence find freedom. I have also never met a man who accidentally stumbled into victory. The proof that a man is fully committed to freedom is whether he is willing to close all the doors to temptation during the beginning stages of repentance.

Solomon closes the story of the young man and the promiscuous woman of Proverbs 7 with this sober warning:

> Do not let your heart turn aside to her ways, do not stray into her paths; For she has cast down many wounded, and all who were slain by her were strong men. Her house is the way to hell, descending to the chambers of death. (vss. 25-27)

Lest any man think he is beyond being tempted by sin, Solomon warns us that the woman in the proverb has slain many strong men. Human history is filled with those who seemed to be strong intellectually, economically, militarily and even spiritually. Nevertheless, many of them have become numbered among those who have fallen to sexual sin. They are the men who refused to do what it takes to close the door to her invitation. For men who truly desire freedom, we need to stop living carelessly like the young man and make the difficult decision to close every door to possible temptation.

In the next chapter, we will examine the spiritual side of the process of repentance that must also be addressed.

CHAPTER 10

Cut:// close-every-door

PRAYER POINTS

- Pray that God will continue to give wisdom to companies that provide protection in the digital world and that they will be able to be stay on top of technological improvements

- Pray for guidance and a willingness to properly close all doors to temptation

- Pray for protection over the young people among your family and friends, that they will be able to avoid exposure and be insulated from porn

DISCUSSION QUESTIONS

1. The opening of the chapter states: "Wherever there is an open door to temptation, it needs to be tightly shut. If a man leaves a door even slightly cracked, the enemy will use that access point to continually lure him back into his sin. Prolonged freedom will never happen if the door is left ajar." Do you agree with this statement? Why or why not?

2. How does the young man in Proverbs 7 relate to the professing Christian in sin?

3. What parallels can you find between the attitude and actions of the immoral woman and the enemy of our souls?

4. Explain in your own words what Jesus meant when He talked about radical amputation. How can a man who wants to get free from porn practically apply His teaching?

5. How could straddling the fence on shutting doors to temptation subvert a man's effort to get free from porn?

PERSONAL APPLICATION QUESTIONS

1. How desperate are you to get free? Are you willing to take radical actions to prevent access to porn?

2. Where are the open doors in your life? Which of the practical suggestions do you need to implement immediately?

3. Who needs to be involved as you walk through this process to make sure you follow through?

Restart:// the-first-works

I N THE PREVIOUS CHAPTER, WE discussed the importance of closing all doors to the enemy to prevent further entanglement with porn. While working on closing those doors to temptation, you need to also take the critical step of opening the door of your heart to the Lord. If the definition of repentance is turning away from sin and toward God, then the opposite is true: The pursuit of sin is essentially turning *away* from Him. Effectively, a door open to sin is a door closed to the Lord.

In case I have not stated it clearly enough, I want to make one point clear: I do not personally believe that true and lasting freedom from sexual sin is possible without an authentic relationship with God through Jesus Christ. I understand that a man can experience abstinence from porn. However, true freedom is a deeper work of the heart that only the Holy Spirit can accomplish. This is why addressing the spiritual life is a vital step in the process. Without it, all the other principles of this book will fall short.

The sobering reality about the heart of a professing Christian addicted to porn is that he is not as close to the Lord as he may imagine himself to be. 1 John 3:6 states, "No one who abides in him keeps on sinning; no one who keeps on sinning has either seen him or known him." (ESV) Chapter 4 provided multiple passages from Scripture that echo this truth. Every man who is involved with pornography needs to conduct a serious evaluation of his true spiritual condition. Paul's advice to the carnal Christians of Corinth should be taken seriously by any professing Christian addicted to porn: "Examine yourselves as to whether you are in the faith."[1]

THE FIRST WORKS

Around the year A.D. 96, the Apostle John found himself in exile on the island of Patmos because of his faith in Christ. It seemed that the enemy had won a victory by banning him into obscurity where his ministry would be significantly hindered. However, the Lord had a specific plan for that season. It was during his banishment that he wrote what we refer to as the Book of Revelation. In the beginning of the book, an angel told John to write a letter from Jesus to seven churches in Asia Minor. To the church in Ephesus, he was instructed to write:

> I know your works, your labor, your patience, and that you cannot bear those who are evil. And you have tested those who say they are apostles and are not, and have found them liars; and you have persevered and have patience, and have labored for My name's sake and have not become weary. Nevertheless I have this against you, that you have left your first love. Remember therefore from where you have fallen; repent and do the first works, or else I will come to you quickly and remove your lampstand from its place—unless you repent. **(Revelation 2:2-5)**

Jesus' desire for every believer is to be on-fire for Him at all times. While that may not be the common experience of everyone in the Western church, that does not make it any less true. He told the Ephesian church to repent and "do the first works." (vs. 5) What that means is simple yet packed with spiritual potential. Jesus admonished them to practice the disciplines that would fuel intimacy in their relationship with Him. The implication is that there were spiritual habits that were part of their pursuit of God that had slipped away in the busyness of church life. Albert Barnes explains:

"It is to engage at once in doing what they did in the first and best days of their piety...Let them read the Bible as they did then; let them pray as they did then; let them go forth in the duties of active benevolence as they did then; let them engage in teaching a Sunday school as they did then; let them relieve the distressed, instruct the ignorant, raise up the fallen, as they did then; let them open their heart, their purse, and their hand, to bless a dying world. As it was in this way that they manifested their love then, so this would be better suited than all other things to rekindle the flame of love when it is almost extinguished."[2]

I can relate to the Ephesian church in my own experience. When I was living a double-life, I was doing a lot of good works. I was leading people to Jesus, working as a missionary, counseling those in need and spreading the Gospel. But the reality of my internal world was much different than it looked on the outside. I would still pray and read the Bible, attend worship services and even preach. However, my intimacy with the Lord was waning because doing the first works requires more than the outward actions alone. They must be done within the context of relational intimacy with the Lord.

The challenge of discussing spiritual disciplines is that they can be done with wrong motives. Jesus addressed this in the Sermon on the Mount when He spoke about prayer and explained that some use it as a public performance or a religious ritual. He said the same about the disciplines of giving and fasting.[3] Essentially, Jesus was warning us that any spiritual discipline that is not grounded in true intimacy with God is nothing more than rote religious exercise.

I know that there are men reading these words who will be tempted to skip this chapter with the thought, "I'm praying and reading the Bible. I'm involved in worship at church. I'm doing everything you are talking about already." But the question is whether we practice these things from a sincere passion for the Lord or out of a sense of guilt, obligation or spiritual pride. The truth is that *if a man was as close to the Lord as he thinks he is, he would not be living in sexual sin.* Jesus said, "If you love Me, keep My commandments."[4] The belief that any Christian can be a passionate follower of Christ and still routinely watch porn is not supported by Scripture.

I want to look at five spiritual disciplines that will have a significant impact in your battle against sexual sin when practiced with a sincere heart. Consider the consistency and quality of each discipline in your life as well as how you can pursue them in a deeper way.

DISCIPLINE 1: PRAYER

Hopefully by now, you realize that willpower alone cannot set you free from porn. Its highly addictive nature cannot be defeated through human effort. We can only find true freedom when a power greater than ourselves is fighting on our side. That power comes from the Holy Spirit and is accessible through intimate prayer.

Prayer has a transactional quality that is not experienced in the physical realm. However, it is very real to the man who develops a true life in God. Something takes place in a man's prayer life that will bolster his strength and enable him to fight spiritual battles with increased vigor. This is something I have experienced countless times in my walk with the Lord. Although I endeavor to spend a substantial time in prayer every day, if I ever miss that time, my disconnection from God manifests in a lack of spiritual vitality and an increase of carnal thinking. Prayer provides a source of spiritual strength and keeps us focused on the Lord.

Paul tells us in 2 Corinthians 10:4 that, "the weapons of our warfare are not carnal but mighty in God for pulling down strongholds." When we spend time seeking the face of God every day, it puts us in connection with three of these potent spiritual weapons.

First, prayer gives us access to the grace of God. Grace is much more than receiving forgiveness for sin. It is also the power given by the Holy

Spirit to enable us to walk in holiness. Paul explains this in his letter to Titus:

> For the grace of God that brings salvation has appeared to all men, teaching us that, denying ungodliness and worldly lusts, we should live soberly, righteously, and godly in the present age...
> **(Titus 2:11-12)**

Here, Paul reveals that grace trains us to deny ungodliness and the lusts of this world. That certainly includes all forms of sexual sin. Any man who desires to live "soberly, righteously and godly" must access the grace of God for the power to do so. Hebrews 4:16 tells us that we can boldly approach the throne of God "that we may obtain mercy and find grace to help in time of need." This is one of the primary reasons that a solid prayer life is vital to walking in freedom. We desperately need the grace of God in our battle to overcome porn and it is made available to us as we seek Him.

The second weapon we receive in prayer is God's peace. Paul speaks about how to access it in his letter to the believers in Philippi:

> Be anxious for nothing, but in everything by prayer and supplication, with thanksgiving, let your requests be made known to God; and the peace of God, which surpasses all understanding, will guard your hearts and minds through Christ Jesus.
> **(Philippians 4:6-7)**

This passage instructs us that God's peace can guard our hearts and minds. The term *guard* is *phroureó*, which means to "keep as by a military guard."[5] One commentary explains, "It implies a sense of active and continuous watchfulness, often in a military or protective context."[6] Any man battling against porn has allowed his heart and mind to be flooded with the filth of sexual sin. He desperately needs to find a way to guard himself against the barrage of thoughts and temptations that are sure to be leveled at him from the enemy. Paul tells us to pray to the Lord so that we can access the peace of God, which acts as a barrier between us and the lure of sexual sin.

The third weapon that prayer provides the child of God is spiritual insulation. Jesus said in Matthew 26:41, "Watch and pray, lest you enter into temptation." Matthew Poole states that in speaking these words to His disciples, Jesus explains, "that it was not in their power to stand without God's help and assistance, which must be obtained by prayer, and upon their praying should not be denied them."[7] To fight this battle victoriously, we need to do whatever it takes to prevent ourselves from succumbing to temptation. We learn from Jesus that there is a direct correlation between our prayer life and our ability to resist the temptations around us. Through our communion with the Lord, we develop the determination, fortitude and desire to say "No" to the sin that has kept us bound. We need to be insulated from temptation, and prayer provides that extra layer of spiritual protection.

How can a struggling man be confident that his prayer life will result in these powerful benefits? From Genesis to Revelation, the Bible reveals that our Creator is a God who answers the prayers of His people:

- John tells us that we can be confident in the Lord "that if we ask anything according to His will, He hears us." **(1 John 5:14)**

- We are told in Jeremiah, "Then you will call upon Me and go and pray to Me, and I will listen to you." **(Jeremiah 29:12)**

- David declares, "The Lord is near to all who call upon Him, to all who call upon Him in truth." **(Psalm 145:18)**

- Scripture also tells us that the Lord is "a rewarder of those who diligently seek Him." **(Hebrews 11:6)**

The Bible repeatedly reminds us of God's desire that His people pray and promises to respond when they do. Any man who thinks he can overcome porn in his own strength is not only fooling himself, but he is also robbing himself of an opportunity for the Lord to join him in his battle.

Prayer is meant to be a daily experience with the Lord where we carve out intentional time to interact with Him. If you are wondering how to begin, the process is simple: Set a time in your daily schedule (preferably in the beginning of your day) where you will commit to spending time with the Lord. There are many ways to spend that time, such as using prayer models from the Bible, praying the Scriptures themselves, worshipping the Lord and bringing requests to Him. However, it is vital that our prayer lives are sincere, consistent and rooted in intimacy with God.

DISCIPLINE 2: SCRIPTURE

Interaction with the truths of Scripture is also essential for the man who desires to delete porn from his life. This discipline must be prioritized for four reasons. First, the Bible has a crucial role in the process of repentance. Psalm 19:7 tells us that "the law of the Lord is perfect, converting the soul." The root of the Hebrew word for *converting* is *shoob* and is the term commonly used in the Old Testament for repentance. Other translations use words such as *reviving* or *restoring*, but the literal translation might sound something like, "repenting the soul." Think about the implications of that statement. Engaging with the Bible is directly linked to experiencing repentance. Studying God's Word is so much more than checking off a box on a spiritual to-do list. When approached with the right attitude it will bring about repentance in our hearts.

Second, the Word of God has the power to radically alter our thought lives. The Apostle Paul exhorts us in Romans 12:2: "Be transformed by the renewing of your mind." This is what the man in sexual sin needs because his internal world has become so distorted and perverted by the satanically inspired images he has given himself over to. To get free, he must be willing to do the difficult work of re-training his mind to think according to God's truth. Too often, we hope for a simple process that will fix all our problems overnight. In reality, most of us have spent years allowing our minds to be impacted and reprogrammed by the sick world of porn. We need to be willing to embrace the sometimes slow and painstaking process of renewing our minds with the truths of Scripture daily.

Third, engaging with the truth of the Bible will result in freedom. Jesus declared in John 8:32 that knowing the truth is what sets us free. A man in bondage to sexual sin needs to encounter the pure, unadulterated truth of God's Word daily because it contains power that can assist us in our spiritual battles. Jesus demonstrated this during His time in the wilderness. Each time Satan approached Him trying to tempt Him away from God's will, Jesus responded with words directly from Scripture. Likewise, any time a man is tempted to embrace a lie from the enemy, the answer is always to fight it with biblical truth. We need to have His Word hidden in our hearts so that we will be prepared when temptation comes.

Fourth, we are told in Scripture that God's Word can help us walk in sexual purity. Psalm 119:9 tells us plainly that the way for a young man to keep his way sexually pure is by "taking heed according to [God's] word." The man in sexual sin has failed to allow the truths of Scripture to guard his purity. However, by applying the precepts of the Bible, we can find our way back to a place of sexual purity and learn how to remain there. If you are serious about walking in purity, you will learn how to guard it with the truth of God's Word.

This is why daily, intentional and meaningful interaction with the Word of God is so essential for us. If we are not filling ourselves with God's truth, we will easily fall for deception and will become a soft target for the enemy. Consider how much deception we have allowed into our lives through the demonic world of pornography. We have embraced lies and meditated on content that goes directly against the truth. The man who sincerely wants to get free from porn will make his time in the Bible a top priority so that he can fill his heart and mind with freedom-producing truth. Make time to interact with the Bible daily and you will reap incredible results in your spiritual life.

DISCIPLINE 3: FASTING

I remember a conversation I had with our pastor a couple years after I had walked through repentance. We were sitting in his office one evening and he asked, "What have you implemented into your life since you graduated from Pure Life that has made the biggest difference?" Without hesitation, one word came out of my mouth: *fasting*.

Fasting is one of the most powerful and effective spiritual tools in helping a man maintain freedom from sexual sin. One of the reasons for this is that it helps to establish self-denial in a man's life. There is no better way to learn how to resist the cravings of the flesh, than to practice saying "No" to its desire for food. Indulging in pornography and sexual sin is the antithesis of fasting. Rather than learning to deny the flesh, it causes us to feed our flesh. Our sinful nature becomes a monster that requires us to continually feed its insatiable appetite. By repeatedly giving over to porn, we are training ourselves to expect constant gratification which affects every other area of our lives. William Law wrote:

"If religion requires us sometimes to fast and to deny our natural appetites, it is to lessen that struggle and war that is in our nature. It is to render our bodies fitter instruments of purity and more obedient to the good motions of divine grace. It is to dry up the springs of our passions that war against the soul, to cool the flame of our blood, and to render the mind more capable of divine meditations."[8]

There are seasons and occasions in which I practice extended fasting. In addition, I have also endeavored to keep in place the practice of fasting on a regular, scheduled basis, a practice I refer to as maintenance fasting. This is usually a one day fast or a partial fast (e.g., skip two meals). My goal is to do this on a weekly basis although I have not always been consistent with it due to how my flesh fights it. It is difficult to describe the spiritual benefits of maintenance fasting because it is easier understood by experience. However, when I am not practicing it consistently, I feel more spiritually apathetic and carnal. My thought life becomes more difficult to control and my overall sensitivity to the Lord slowly wanes. I find that fighting lust is more of a challenge and my overall attitude becomes more self-focused. When I fast, it is like layers of hardness around my heart are cut away and my intimacy with the Lord is restored. While it is hard to explain, one thing I know for sure: Any man who is hooked on porn needs to do whatever he can to reduce the strength of his flesh and allow his spiritual man to gain control in his life.

This is why one key to overcoming is to start implementing maintenance fasting right away. You will have to discover what works best for you. There is no question that fasting has helped me immeasurably to resist temptation, crucify the flesh and walk in the Spirit. In fact, Jesus taught His disciples that some spirits could only be overcome through prayer and fasting.[9] This tells me that some spiritual strongholds can only be broken through regular fasting. Beyond that, Scripture implies that fasting can move the heart of God.[10] Fasting certainly has an impact on the efficacy of prayer. The man who is addicted to sin should practice fasting on a regular basis if he wants to experience deliverance.

DISCIPLINE 4: WORSHIP

The quality of our worship speaks volumes about our spiritual condition. When I use the word *worship*, I am not referring to how well someone can recite lyrics on Sunday or how loudly he might belt them out. Worship involves a lifestyle that exalts God and places Him first in every facet of life even beyond the worship service.

Humans were created with the drive to worship something. It is a God-given function that is part of our original design. And this longing to worship was meant to lead us into relationship with our Creator. However, history has proven that many take the worship that belongs to God and instead redirect it toward people and objects in this world.

Paul described this process in Romans 1 when he wrote about the cycle of human depravity. Interestingly, he uses sexual sin as his primary illustration. Within that context, he says that people "exchanged the truth of God for the lie, and worshiped and served the creature rather than the Creator." (vs. 25) What an apt description of the man who claims to love God but is given over to pornography!

Many reading these words have been guilty of lifting their voices to the Lord in church on Sunday yet are full of guilt and shame because of ongoing secret sin throughout the week. Sensing God's presence in church can actually help deceive a man into thinking he is in right fellowship with the Lord. Yet, it is very possible that the Lord would say to them what He told the Jewish people of His day: "These people draw near to Me with their mouth, and honor Me with their lips, but their heart is far from Me."[11]

Sexual sin is the equivalent of spiritual idolatry. It is a god that you have allowed to consume your time, attention and money. Every time you indulge in sexual sin, you are bowing your knees at its altar and stealing the allegiance that God alone deserves in your life. As Steve Gallagher puts it, through sexual sin our "sexuality and capacity to worship become fused into a corrupted, nearly irresistible drive to worship at the altar of sexual idolatry."[12]

By developing a lifestyle of *true* worship, a man can learn how to shift his focus off the things of this world and onto the Lord. This is what you need more than anything: a true sight of Jesus! It is only as you look upon Him that freedom will begin to take root in your life. As you are walking through the process of deleting porn from your life, it is important to evaluate your personal worship of God and ask Him to restore a heart of true worship in your life.

DISCIPLINE 5: SHOWING MERCY

Mercy is a concept that is interwoven throughout Scripture. Perhaps one of the most well-known verses about mercy is Micah 6:8: "He has shown you, O man, what is good; and what does the Lord require of you but to do justly, to love mercy, and to walk humbly with your God?" We often think of mercy exclusively in terms of God's willingness to refrain from giving us what we deserve. However, that mercy that we received from Him is meant to be shown through us as we in turn give it to others.

The power of showing mercy may seem unrelated to ridding porn from our lives, but it is actually a very powerful tool for the man who wants to get free. One story that illustrates this is a conversation that Jesus had with a Pharisee in Luke 11. In response to the Pharisee's shock that Jesus had not performed a socially expected handwashing ritual before eating, Jesus spoke the following words:

Now you Pharisees make the outside of the cup and dish clean, but your inward part is full of greed and wickedness. Foolish ones! Did not He who made the outside make the inside also? But rather give alms of such things as you have; then indeed all things are clean to you. (vss. 39-41)

What Jesus is prescribing to the religious leaders of His day might not make much sense at first glance. How could giving money away have anything to do with their internal heart issues? The problem according to Jesus was their greed and wickedness, which seems disconnected from their outward actions. However, what is being suggested is a very practical way to reverse the flow of their internal lives. Jesus was explaining that if the Pharisees would become givers, rather than takers, their lives could be transformed. Rex Andrews explains:

"This is the opposite to the defiling process…a purifying process. The evil heart pours out that which defiles the man. The good heart pours out that which purifies the man…What does the new heart do which purifies instead of defiles? Gives that which it has received: Mercy."[13]

As we discussed in Chapter 5, one of the negative consequences of pornography is that it fuels lust for people. Lust is a selfish desire to have something that does not belong to us. Every time we look upon a woman lustfully, whether in a picture, on a screen or passing by, we are trying to take something from her that is not ours to take. She is another man's daughter, sister or perhaps wife. To lust upon a woman is to presume upon her innocence and even when it is done internally, it is an unwelcome intrusion into her life. It is a shame that many men can so freely indulge in lustful thoughts without the slightest feeling of guilt about it.

Pure Life Ministries taught me one of the most practical disciplines to fight off a lustful spirit, which is to pray that God will have mercy on anyone that I am tempted to lust over. What takes place internally when you pray for someone is that you are intentionally giving to that person, which is the opposite function of taking from them. Again, from Rex Andrews:

"The Mercy-ing prayer turns the 'look' from lusting to giving help; from destroying virtue to giving life and freedom and hope. The adulterous spirit is a lying, cheating, stealing, destroyer of truth and virtue and hope and faith, and the violator and ruiner and poisoner of love. But the Spirit and prayer of Mercy is a saving, life-giving, truth of faith and hope and virtue by which the true love of God can protect, bless, strengthen, preserve, fulfill all need. Pray then, when you are tempted in this way, until the grip of faith comes, 'Flood that one I am looking at in my heart and mind, with fulfilling mercies...As you have mercied me, so mercy her, or him.'"[14]

The man who will begin to practice this simple discipline in his daily life, will not only find the power of his lust being conquered, but will also experience an intimacy with the Lord that cannot be found any other way. Jesus is concerned about the souls of every man and woman in the world. When we join Him in His pursuit of souls, rather than constantly trying to steal a glance or thought about others, we will experience His presence in a special way.***

THE POWER OF PUTTING
FIRST THINGS FIRST

A critical component of this process of repentance is getting the most essential relationship we have back in order. Jesus told the church in Ephesus that they had forsaken their first love. They were doing some good things but not from a place of intimacy. He called them to return to Him through repentance by doing the "first works." Based on the five disciplines discussed in this chapter, what are those first works that you need to implement into your life? If you once walked closely with the Lord, what sorts of things were you practicing that sexual sin has caused you to forsake? I am not suggesting that you develop a complex strategy that feels like an overwhelming mountain. I am talking about simple things that you

---

*** See Appendix B for a format on how to pray for mercy.

can implement right now. Even the smallest efforts toward these spiritual disciplines will reap powerful spiritual benefits in your life. Intimacy with God is a catalyst for freedom from sexual sin. Doing what it takes to develop that intimacy is a game-changer in the battle against porn.

In the next chapter, we are going to talk about a very important step that you can take on the road to freedom. It involves allowing the Scriptures to do what they do best: confront our hearts and offer a different way of living.

CHAPTER 11

Restart:// the-first-works

PRAYER POINTS

- Pray for a spiritual renewal to take place in your life as you seek to engage with the spiritual disciplines in this chapter

- Pray for a spiritual revival to take place in churches throughout the nation, returning us to our first love corporately

- Pray that your pastor and other spiritual leaders in your life will experience a fresh outpouring of intimacy with God

DISCUSSION QUESTIONS

1. Explain in your own words what Jesus is encouraging the church in Ephesus to do. How might that apply to the modern American church?

2. Are there other spiritual disciplines not addressed in this chapter that you think would provide further intimacy with God and insulation from temptation?

3. What is the connection between praying for others and freedom from lust? What are some practical ways to implement this discipline into a man's life?

4. How does a man identify and rid his life of idols? Do you think this is a common problem for all Christians? Why or why not?

5. The following statement is in this chapter: "The truth is that if a man was as close to the Lord as he thinks he is, he would not be living in sexual sin." Do you agree? What biblical evidence can you find to support or refute that statement?

PERSONAL APPLICATION QUESTIONS

1. Which of the five disciplines listed in this chapter are the weakest in your life? What about the strongest? How can you grow in the areas that you need to work on?

2. Do you see a lack of true intimacy in your prayer and devotional life? How has sexual sin contributed to that lack?

3. How often have you engaged with the discipline of fasting and how can you take it to the next level in your spiritual life?

12

Help:// seek-counsel

W HEN I CONSIDER MY PERSONAL journey, I have experienced prolonged seasons of freedom from porn twice. The first was during the year I spent in Teen Challenge at eighteen years old. While a year may not sound very impressive to some, at that time, every day that I was able to stay out of bondage seemed like a miracle. Unfortunately, that season ended prematurely due to my sinful decisions. The second began in 2011 when I went through Pure Life Ministries which continues to this day. When I look for parallels between those two seasons, one obvious element is the effectiveness of the biblical counsel I received in both programs. In fact, biblical truth has been monumental in my life every time I have applied it in my battle against sexual sin.

While the previous chapter addressed your need to prioritize your vertical relationship with God in the pursuit of freedom, in this chapter, I want to focus on an important horizontal relationship that needs to be established. You need to form a one-on-one counseling relationship with a spiritually mature man who can confront and encourage you with the Word of God.

CONFRONTED WITH TRUTH

A man who wants to walk in total freedom from sexual sin must deal with the deception that he has allowed into his life. The most effective way of overcoming the lies of the enemy is for a godly man to expose them for what they are and counter them with biblical truth. The Scriptures have unmatched power to set men free from life-controlling issues. Before we talk about establishing a biblical counseling relationship, we will first examine three principles about the nature of the Bible that make it such a reliable and effective way to experience life transformation.

PRINCIPLE #1:
The Bible is the Word of God

The Bible testifies that it is a book completely distinct from any other collection of writings. It declares, "All Scripture is God-breathed"[1] and that it was inspired by the Holy Spirit.[2] In other words, its wisdom is more than what human authors can contrive. In addition, Hebrews 4:12 says it is "alive and active." Whatever a person thinks about the Scriptures, one thing that everyone should be able to agree on is that the Bible clearly presents itself as something more than an ordinary book. Any author can assert lofty things about his writing, but that does not necessarily make his claims true. The Bible, on the other hand, has produced countless testimonies of its ability to transform lives over hundreds of years.

As we have discussed throughout this book, pornography is not only a biological problem, but, more importantly, a spiritual problem. Sexual sin is an issue that only God can fix because of its spiritual nature. It is true that porn affects a man biologically, socially and psychologically. However, if he only addresses those aspects and fails to deal with the spiritual nature of his sin, he will rob himself of the most powerful weapon available which is *repentance*. As Paul states, "The sting of death is sin, and the strength of sin is the law. But thanks be to God, who gives us the victory through our Lord Jesus Christ."[3] And in Romans, "O wretched man that I am! Who will deliver me from this body of death? I thank God—through Jesus Christ our Lord!"[4] The man who wants to experience true victory in his life, not only from porn, but from the power of sin itself, must look to the principles of God's Word.

PRINCIPLE #2:

The Bible Contains Life-Changing Wisdom

If God orchestrated and inspired the writing and assembly of the sixty-six books of the Bible as a means of revealing Himself to the human race, then what is contained therein must be extremely important for us. If the Bible contains God's wisdom for us, then it can be expected to be sufficient to address every problem that you and I can experience in this life. We know that He gave the Bible to mankind at least in part to teach us how to live wisely on the earth.

While the Bible is a collection of many styles of writing, the emphasis it places on moral instruction cannot be overlooked. Even the narrative portions of Scripture provide obvious principles to show us what it means to walk in wisdom and righteousness before the Lord. Much of the Bible contains explicit instruction, such as the Wisdom Literature of the Old Testament, Jesus' Sermon on the Mount and Paul's instructions to the early church. The Scriptures clearly intend to teach us how to apply godly wisdom to our lives.

The Bible contrasts God's wisdom and man's wisdom throughout its pages. The Lord spoke the following words through the prophet Isaiah: "As the heavens are higher than the earth, so are my ways higher than your ways and my thoughts than your thoughts."[5] While man's wisdom is limited, temporal and corrupted by sin, God's wisdom is unlimited, eternal and pure. When we live according to His wisdom, we will enjoy the blessings and peace of God in our lives. Martin Luther once said, "I am content with this gift of the Scriptures, which teaches and supplies all that is necessary, both for this life and that which is to come."[6] Human wisdom got us into the predicament that we found ourselves in when we realized that porn had a grip on our hearts that we could not escape. By turning to the Bible, we can begin to walk in God's wisdom, which results in righteousness and freedom.

When the wisdom of Scripture is sincerely applied to a life, the outcome will be spiritual transformation. Merely acknowledging the Bible as God's Word containing His wisdom is only the first step of the process. The Bible must then be studied and obeyed to have any transformative effect on one's heart. However, the way that we approach the Scriptures will have a significant impact on that process. Transformation requires that we approach the Word of God with humility and an open heart. We need to respond to the truths it contains with a willingness to put into practice the principles that are revealed. When we do this with the right motivation, the changes that can take place are nothing short of miraculous. And this process of transformation is available, not only in the area of freedom from porn, but for every issue that you and I could face. C.H. Spurgeon made the following observation about the Scriptures:

"You cannot be in a condition that the Word of God has not provided...You will find it unfailing in all periods of your life, in all circumstances, in all companies, in all trials, and under all difficulties. Were it fallible, it would be useless in emergencies, but its unerring truth renders it precious beyond all price to the soldiers of the cross."[7]

If you and I had truly lived our lives within the wisdom of the Bible, we would never have ended up bound to pornography. It contains a myriad of warnings within its pages regarding the danger of stepping outside of God's boundaries in the sexual arena. Psalm 119 explains that the way a man can stay pure is by living according to the wisdom of God's Word.[8] Proverbs is filled with admonitions to avoid sexual sin.[9] Song of Solomon provides the proper context in which to enjoy sex. Jesus spoke about lust and warned us to avoid it.[10] Paul gave warnings about sexual immorality and its danger in several of his epistles.[11] If we had put into practice the precepts of Scripture, we would have been able to make decisions that would have kept us away from all forms of sexual sin.

PRINCIPLE #3:

The Bible Encourages Mutual Accountability

The New Testament was written in the context of a community of believers. There is something to be said about the importance of growing spiritually within a communal context. In fact, many of the commands of Scripture assume relationship with other people. For example, a Christian cannot obey the following Scriptures outside of relationships with others:

- Be kind to one another, tenderhearted, forgiving one another, even as God in Christ forgave you. **(Ephesians 4:32)**

- This is My commandment, that you love one another as I have loved you. **(John 15:12)**

- Just as you want men to do to you, you also do to them likewise. **(Luke 6:31)**

- Be kindly affectionate to one another with brotherly love, in honor giving preference to one another. **(Romans 12:10)**

- Finally, all of you be of one mind, having compassion for one another; love as brothers, be tenderhearted, be courteous… **(1 Peter 3:8)**

- Let each of you look out not only for his own interests, but also for the interests of others. **(Philippians 2:4)**

The expectation of the New Testament is that Christians will live their lives in the context of a spiritual community. Doing so creates a sense of accountability when someone in the church acts in a way contrary to the teaching of Scripture.

In Western society, we sometimes have difficulty grasping this concept because we typically approach the Bible from an individualistic perspective. It is not uncommon in our culture to hear someone share what a Scripture verse means to him personally, often taking it completely out of context. We are experiencing a disturbing trend of professing Christians who think they can live for God outside of a Christian community. This type of me-and-God-alone approach would be foreign to the early church.

While the thrust of this chapter is about finding mutual accountability in a relationship with a counselor, it is worth mentioning here that all of us need to be in meaningful relationships with other believers. There is a special protection experienced when we are an active and engaged participant in a local church. It provides a covering of prayer as well as a sense of belonging. If you are disconnected from a church body, it is time to reconnect and find a Bible-preaching church where you can get plugged in. Staying connected to the Body of Christ is an important support system that a man needs in his life.

However, it should also be noted that merely attending a church does not qualify as being an active part of its community. While some have opted out of church completely under the guise of "I don't need organized religion to walk with God," others are in church every week and yet are not truly under the spiritual covering of their pastors and the church community. This is unfortunately common in the American church, where warming a seat on Sunday is often equated with belonging to a faith community. That could not be further from the culture of the New Testament Body of Christ. If you have not experienced the blessing of being involved in a true community of believers, I suggest you meet with your pastor and ask how you can become more engaged in your church and come under the spiritual covering of the body.

Because the truths of the Bible need to be correctly and sincerely applied to bring spiritual transformation, a man should never approach this process alone. Although repentance takes place in the heart between a man and God, the process of repentance requires accountability with other people. Most men reading these words already have some level of understanding of the Bible. In fact, they have probably read much of its contents, studied Scripture-based books and heard countless sermons preached. Yet, they still allowed themselves to live in a way that is contrary to biblical truth because there was no one holding them accountable to obey what they were reading. This is why submission to another man who can provide biblical counsel is a necessary part of the repentance process.

FINDING BIBLICAL COUNSEL

Most prideful men will resist the thought of submitting themselves to counseling. They have the mistaken belief that they should be able to do everything alone and that reaching out for help is a display of weakness. I would counter this type of thinking by suggesting that one quality of a true man of God is having the humility to pursue help when he needs it. Although one's flesh will rail against it, there are seasons in our lives when we need someone to come alongside us, take us by the hand and teach us how to walk in freedom.

Before I went to Pure Life Ministries, I sought help through a variety of counseling methods. I went to a Christian psychologist, but we spent most of our time digging into my past, which only gave me the impression that there were others to blame for my problems. I submitted myself to a psychiatrist who put me on anti-anxiety medication. While I had high hopes that the pills were going to fix everything, instead, they only succeeded in numbing my emotions. I also tried a Christian twelve-step program, where I would share my latest sinful activity in a group setting. It helped me appease my conscience because I was confessing my sin, yet I remained in bondage. The bottom line is that I found no freedom in any of these places. What I needed was a confrontation with the truth of God's Word, not a pep-talk, pill or a false sense of piety.

I am not saying that these avenues cannot help people. I know men who have had a measure of success in their lives through therapy and twelve-step programs. However, any type of counseling that does not have the Word of God as its foundation will fail to truly confront sin and therefore cannot address the spiritual dynamic of sexual addiction. While a man does need encouragement along the way, a pat on the back will not bring him into freedom.

For the man hooked on pornography, the goal is not simply to get him to stop looking at it. That might be a step in the right direction, but he can stop looking at porn and still go to hell. He can stop the outward action and still be corrupt within. Sexual sin is like a cancer to the soul of a man. Even if he never looks at another pornographic image the rest of his life, that does not mean he is truly free inside. But if he is set free by the Lord, as Jesus tells us, he will "be free indeed."[12] Then his outward behavior will line up with his *internal* state. This is why a man in sexual sin needs the power of the Word of God and the Holy Spirit to do a deep internal work of repentance to truly find freedom. The best that secular counseling can do is try to help modify a person's thinking and behavior. However, God can transform a person from the inside out.

Let us now consider three options for inviting a godly man into your life who knows how to use Scripture to assist you in the process of life-transformation. This relationship is one that should be established immediately. A counseling relationship is meant to be temporary and will typically be discontinued as you learn how to walk in freedom.

Certified Biblical Counselors

There are several organizations with certified counselors who are trained to help people properly apply the Word of God to their lives. I have personally sought out professional biblical counsel over the years for help with stressful situations, marital problems and other issues I have faced. I know many others who have done the same and have experienced dramatic transformation. A good biblical counselor will teach you how to search the Scriptures, apply them to your situation and will walk alongside you for a season until you have the strength to stand on your own.

One benefit of utilizing a counselor who has been licensed with a particular biblical organization is that you can trust that they have been trained and vetted. The vetting process they go through includes accountability regarding their theological and philosophical beliefs as well their counseling methods. It is worth the time to research the values and theological statements of an organization before reaching out for a counselor. Also, keep in mind that if you cannot find a biblical counselor physically near you, online or phone counseling is also possible with some organizations.

A biblical counselor will be able to describe in advance the process that he employs to walk men into freedom, including the frequency of meetings, overall time-frame and any resources he uses. While most charge a fee for their counseling, it is typically far less than a psychotherapist charges. Be that as it may, any investment that you make towards your freedom is worth it. If you have never experienced solid biblical counseling, I strongly recommend finding a certified counselor and allowing him to join you on your journey into freedom.***

Pastoral Counselors

While not every pastor is certified in biblical counseling, many understand how to teach people to apply the truths of Scripture to their lives. Pastors are in a unique situation in that they deal with a variety of people in many circumstances. This gives them a broad perspective and the ability to walk with people through many of life's challenges, including sexual sin. Before entering into a counseling relationship with a minister, ask some pointed questions to determine if it is a good fit for your situation, such as:

- What are your views on the sufficiency of Scripture to help me get free from pornography?

- How long are you able to commit to meeting with me and how will we know when that season has ended?

- Have you seen other men you have counseled get free from porn?

There is nothing wrong with asking direct questions, as this relationship is one that should have a significant impact on your journey. If the answers do not line up with your expectations, seek out someone else who can walk

---

***For a list of specific biblical counseling organizations, see Appendix C

with you. Many churches offer counseling as a service, so you can most likely find options in your area if you do some research. Pastors who are gifted in counseling can be a great source of blessing to a man who wants to delete porn from his life.

Mature Believers

While finding someone with training and experience in biblical counseling has many advantages, what should you do if you cannot locate a trained professional? One option is to find a trusted brother in Christ who has spiritual maturity in his life and ask him to help walk you through the process of repentance. Appendix F provides a framework for what that process could look like on a practical level. A mature believer will have learned over his lifetime how to overcome many personal challenges by applying God's Word. He can provide a counseling-type relationship where you are held accountable for your response to the Scriptures and can lovingly confront you when it is necessary along the way.

Just like with a professional or pastoral counselor, a specific time frame and clear expectations should be laid out in advance. The purpose of biblical counseling is to teach the counselee how to walk according to the Word of God without requiring long-term counseling. Therefore, seeking biblical counsel is an urgent but temporary step in the repentance process. I cannot emphasize enough how effective biblically based counsel can be in your journey. Looking someone in the eye on a regular basis could be the very thing that will help initiate the breakthrough that you have been hoping for before you picked up this book. Take the time before progressing to the next chapter to do some research and prayerfully consider who will be the man you invite into your situation in this critical part of your repentance process.

In the next chapter, we are going to dive deeper into the importance of setting up effective boundaries in your life that can assist in preserving your freedom from porn.

CHAPTER 12

Help:// seek-counsel

PRAYER POINTS

- Pray for the protection and fruitfulness of biblical counselors and organizations worldwide, as they are often under attack by secular governments

- Pray that the Body of Christ will return to a wholehearted commitment to biblical truth wherever it has strayed from it

- Pray that the Lord will lead you to the right man who can lovingly confront you with the Word of God in a way that produces the fruit of repentance

DISCUSSION QUESTIONS

1. This chapter makes the following statement: "It is true that porn affects a man biologically, socially and psychologically. However, if he only addresses those aspects and fails to deal with the spiritual aspect of his sin, he will rob himself of the most powerful weapon available which is repentance." What does this mean for programs and counseling that are not based on Scripture?

2. What is the significance of experiencing transformation inwardly rather than focusing on changing outward behaviors?

3. From your perspective, is the modern church operating primarily from a "Scripture alone" model or one that has embraced human wisdom in how it teaches and preaches? What specifically leads you to think that way?

4. What ramifications should the communal nature of the New Testament have on the modern Christian? How might our experience in Western culture differ from the original setting of the New Testament?

5. What would cause a man to resist being confronted with Scripture, even if it could be the pathway to his freedom?

PERSONAL APPLICATION QUESTIONS

1. Which of the five disciplines listed in this chapter are the weakest in your life? What about the strongest? How can you grow in the areas that you need to work on?

2. Do you see a lack of true intimacy in your prayer and devotional life? How has sexual sin contributed to that lack?

3. How often have you engaged with the discipline of fasting and how can you take it to the next level in your spiritual life?

PART FOUR://

the-ongoing-solution

13

Control:// build-a-wall

THE LAST FOUR CHAPTERS PROVIDED the steps that must be taken to initiate the practical side of the repentance process. If a man wants to delete porn from his life, he must expose his sin, close all doors to temptation, re-establish his spiritual disciplines and find someone to provide biblical counseling. Those four steps make up the immediate process that will get a man pointed in the right direction so that he can make his initial separation from porn. The next four chapters will provide steps to promote ongoing victory in the battle.

Chapter 10 explained the process of closing the doors to porn. In this chapter, I want to elaborate on the topic of ongoing boundaries in our lives to reinforce freedom once we are making progress on our journey. The reality is that we live in a spiritual war zone. There are forces around us that want to destroy our faith, lure us into sin and keep us away from the Kingdom. Our three primary enemies are Satan, the world system and our sinful flesh. These three opponents are continuously working together to destroy our relationship with God. In order to protect ourselves from the temptations that seem to be everywhere, we need to build a strong wall of protection around our lives.

THE SAFETY OF LIVING IN BOUNDARIES

One of the reasons I have been able to walk in freedom for so long is because of the personal boundaries I have set in place. What I have essentially done is secure myself inside a safety fence. If I wanted to view pornography today, it would take a lot of effort and risk on my part. I would have to find access to the internet on an unprotected device or go to an adult bookstore. I intentionally put these boundaries in place to remove the enemy's ability to tempt me back into sin.

While some might think that a life with such strict boundaries is not true freedom, I contend that the Bible is a book of boundaries. When we live within those boundaries, we are truly free. Freedom does not mean that I can sit in a dark room in front of a computer with unlimited access to the internet without anyone knowing—all the while hoping to not look at porn. Instead, a life of freedom means doing whatever it takes to keep porn deleted from my life.

It is important for us to realize that our sinful nature will never change in this life. Our flesh is not converted when we are born again. It will continue to want the exact same sin it has always wanted. This is why there will never be a time in our lives that we are not susceptible to temptation. It is also why Jesus told us to crucify ourselves by taking up a cross[1] and Paul talked so much about taking off the old self and putting on the new one.[2] The flesh will remain part of us until we pass into eternity, so our need for boundaries is lifelong.

I should add that I am not sitting around, white-knuckling, trying to keep myself from viewing porn. That was my miserable situation prior to my repentance. Today, pornography is no longer an issue in my life. Have I ever been tempted? Yes. Do I need to be very careful about my use of the internet? Yes. But this is not a continuous, daily battle anymore. There are times when I experience thoughts and urges, but those are isolated and out of the ordinary. The boundaries that I subject myself to do not inhibit my life but actually serve to promote freedom in it.

BUILDING A WALL OF PROTECTION

Within this context of establishing boundaries, I want to talk about what it looks like to have a strong wall of protection around your heart and life. We will reflect on the story of Nehemiah, who was used by God to rebuild the wall around Jerusalem during the time of Israel's exile. There are five principles from Nehemiah's response to that situation that apply to our own need for a protective wall.

PRINCIPLE #1:

Nehemiah Was Concerned About the Wall

They said to me, "Those who survived the exile and are back in the province are in great trouble and disgrace. The wall of Jerusalem is broken down, and its gates have been burned with fire." When I heard these things, I sat down and wept. For some days I mourned and fasted and prayed before the God of heaven. **(Nehemiah 1:3-4 NIV)**

In the beginning of Nehemiah's story, someone reported to him that the wall of Jerusalem had been reduced to rubble. Something took place in his heart that day that initiated a series of important events. He responded to the news by fasting, weeping and praying about the defenseless city. Nehemiah could have experienced many different reactions. As the official cupbearer of King Artaxerxes, he probably had access to more luxuries than any other Israelite. He could have had the attitude, "Why are you telling me about Jerusalem? I've started over in Persia. Things are pretty good for me. That's someone else's problem to worry about." Instead, he was heartbroken over it, and that led him to take personal responsibility for its rebuilding.

What Nehemiah displayed was the forming of conviction. For the man who wants to stay free from pornography, it will take the same kind of inward determination to ensure that effective boundaries are placed around his heart and life to keep sexual sin at bay. Building a wall of spiritual defense begins by developing a genuine concern over it. I hope after coming this far along the journey that you no longer need to be convinced about the importance of staying free. If you make a half-hearted attempt at creating strong boundaries in your life, you will have the spiritual equivalent of a wall made of cardboard. From the outside, it might look solid, but the enemy will be able to knock it down with little effort.

In contrast, Scripture encourages us to make sure that we keep watch over our hearts. Proverbs 4:23 says, "Above all else, guard your heart, for everything you do flows from it." (NIV) This verse provides the illustration of an armed guard standing watch over a castle entrance, keeping enemies out and providing safety for those within. This is to be the posture of every man of God. Guarding our heart needs to be a priority above everything else in life. A nonchalant attitude will not keep our walls from being breached. We must develop a strong conviction about the need to protect ourselves.

PRINCIPLE #2:

Nehemiah Examined the Condition of the Wall

I went to Jerusalem...By night I went out through the Valley Gate...examining the walls of Jerusalem, which had been broken down, and its gates, which had been destroyed by fire. (Nehemiah 2:11, 13 NIV)

Once Nehemiah arrived in Jerusalem with the resources and people required, the next step was an examination of the wall's condition. He needed to understand exactly what damage had been done, which areas needed the most attention and what types of resources were to be allocated. Repairing and constructing a wall takes intentional preparation. This was a major project as the wall around the city of Jerusalem was about two and a half miles long.[3]

This is foundational for any man who desires to build a wall of protection around himself. He needs to conduct a thorough examination of his overall lifestyle. If you are following the process outlined in this book, you should be coming to this chapter with at least some kind of a wall in place regarding things like technology. That might include limited internet usage, password protected devices, accountability software or even removing devices from your life completely. It is time to make a more thorough assessment of the strength of your wall of protection, not only in the area of technology, but more broadly in your lifestyle. The devil will use any avenue he can to get you to live in compromise. Once he accomplishes that, it will be easier to tempt you with sexual sin because your guard will be down. Here are two areas to consider:

Entertainment

As we have discussed, we live in a lust-driven, sensuous culture. In some ways, it is inescapable. In fact, a report that was written about consumerism estimated that the average American is exposed to a mind-boggling 6,000 to 10,000 advertisements every day![4] Many of these are sexual in nature. While we cannot control some of the stimuli we are exposed to, there are factors that we can limit or eliminate that will help to remove many of these sexual triggers from our lives.

Entertainment can be a huge stumbling block for those who want to keep their minds pure. Hollywood rarely produces any content without a sexual scene, erotic love story or scantily clad body in it. TV shows and even commercials always seem to have a sensual twist. Video games can also be a source of temptation, as so much content is geared toward the flesh. Some games even include blatant nudity and sexual situations. One might say, "But I can't control any of those things. I'm not in charge of the media companies." It is true that we have no control over what they produce, but we definitely have control over what we consume.

When I came home from Pure Life Ministries, our family got rid of secular entertainment including TV connections. While I should mention that my motivation in doing so was not completely related to staying free from sexual sin, this effort to consecrate our lives to the Lord has absolutely helped to prioritize purity. Once in a while, I am in a waiting room at a local business and the TV is on. I am repeatedly shocked at the amount of sexually stimulating materials that are becoming commonplace. I am extremely grateful that I am not exposed to this type of entertainment in my home. Any secular streaming services or TV connections are only inviting spiritual compromise. In response, there are companies like Pure Flix who offer family-friendly and faith-based content that filters out much of the immorality so common in entertainment. The man who wants to maintain purity should not be subjecting himself to everything this world has to offer. He needs to develop a consecrated lifestyle that limits his exposure to the ungodly world of entertainment.

Personal Relationships

While we have primarily talked about pornography thus far, it is important to mention that a protective wall must also include boundaries in relationships. I have met many men who once walked in freedom but were derailed by forming an immoral relationship. Whether you are single or married, how you interact with the opposite sex can cause a breach in your wall of protection that can have devastating consequences.

In order to protect our marriage, I have made a commitment with my wife. We do not allow ourselves to be in a situation where we are alone with someone of the opposite sex. This is for two reasons. First, we never want to give the appearance of impropriety. If someone were to see me eating lunch alone with another woman or my wife at a coffee shop with a man, even if it was innocent in nature, it might give the impression of immorality. The second reason is that neither of us want to put ourselves into a situation where we could be tempted. The reality is that almost all adulterous affairs begin with some kind of emotional connection. The best way to prevent that from happening is to never open a door to it.

Most immoral sexual relationships that single men fall into start the same way. The safest way to avoid ending up in bed with someone is to stop yourself from entering a close physical relationship with them in the first place. Couples who are dating should have strict boundaries in place to help them avoid giving over to sin, even during the engagement process. Unmarried men should also be careful to never be in a potentially compromising situation with women.

Living a life free from the power of lust is a bigger concept than simply cutting out porn. Consider the following questions to get an idea of the effectiveness of your current protection. If you are married, this process should be discussed with your spouse because it will affect everyone in the home.

- In what areas of my life am I allowing the world system to have influence? (Technology, music, books, politics, news, TV, movies, social media, video games, etc.)

  * What potential open doors to immoral content exist in each?

  * Is there any sexual content in what I am watching, listening to, reading or surfing?

  * What is my current relationship with social media and is it influencing my purity in a negative way?

  * Which activities in my life are pulling me away from God and which are pushing me closer to Him?

- If the devil wanted to destroy my purity, what would be his best opportunity based on my current lifestyle?

- What is the spiritual atmosphere of my home and how can I make it more of a sanctuary for the Lord?

- What devices do I have access to with an internet connection? (phones, computers, tablets, laptops, smart watches, kids tech, television, game systems, etc.)

    * Am I properly protecting all these devices through hardware or software as suggested in Chapter 10?

- Are there places I am physically going that are sources of temptation? (gyms, beaches, etc.)

- Are there any areas of my life where I am experiencing temptation to cross an emotional or physical line with another person?

- If I was to rate the current effectiveness of my wall of protection on a scale from 1 to 10, what would it be? (1 being "I have basically no boundaries at all" and 10 being "I am 100% confidence that my wall is unbreachable")

Taking the time to prayerfully consider the effectiveness of your boundaries is crucial for insulating your life from compromise. It is important that you do not answer these questions based on your personal preferences or comfort. As stated before, your freedom from sexual sin is the greatest matter of concern. Any sacrifice to have more of the Lord in your life will always be worth it.

PRINCIPLE #3:

Nehemiah Constructed the Wall

Then I said to them, "You see the trouble we are in: Jerusalem lies in ruins, and its gates have been burned with fire. Come, let us rebuild the wall of Jerusalem, and we will no longer be in disgrace." …They replied, "Let us start rebuilding." So they began this good work. **(Nehemiah 2:17-18 NIV)**

Now that Nehemiah had inspected the condition of the wall, the time came to build and fortify it. Without this step, all the concern and examination would be wasted, nothing more than good intentions. He had to put in the energy, effort and resources to construct the wall that he had drafted in his blueprints.

This is where building boundaries can be challenging. Protective walls are a blessing in that they keep unwanted influences out of our lives. However, those boundaries come with occasional obstacles. For example, I recently had to contact our accountability software company to fix a calendar issue it created on my phone. The software was preventing it from syncing and almost resulted in me missing two meetings. Several times, I have been in businesses that required me to go to an internet browser for their service and I have had to awkwardly explain that I cannot access the internet on my device. These are the types of annoyances that become a normal pattern of life for the man who values freedom over convenience. Sometimes, these situations are comical and other times they are the cause of a lot of frustration or embarrassment. However, keeping our hearts free from bondage makes it well worth it.

Whatever you have discovered in the examination phase creates the blueprint for the wall you are building. In this phase, you should be concerned about more than just the short-term; you want to put a system in place that will last a *lifetime*. Building a strong wall of protection is going to change your lifestyle. There is no way around it. This is where priorities need to be considered and where your true willingness to place the Kingdom above your comforts will be tested.

This is the part of the journey that radically altered the lifestyle of our family. It caused us to become more concerned about making our home a sanctuary than pursuing the pleasures of the world. To put it simply, you cannot expect your lifestyle to remain the same as when you were hooked on porn. Things need to change, and it is more involved than simply blocking porn from your devices. *A man who continues a lifestyle centered around selfish pleasure is setting himself up to return to his sexual sin.*

PRINCIPLE #4:

Nehemiah Protected the Wall

They all plotted together to come and fight against Jerusalem and stir up trouble against it but we prayed to our God and posted a guard day and night to meet this threat…Therefore I stationed some of the people behind the lowest points of the wall at the exposed places, posting them by families, with their swords, spears and bows. After I looked things over, I stood up and said to the nobles, the officials and the rest of the people, "Don't be afraid of them. Remember the Lord, who is great and awesome, and fight for your families, your sons and your daughters, your wives and your homes." **(Nehemiah 4:8-9, 13-14 NIV)**

I love this part of Nehemiah's story. Due to the continued threat the people faced from those opposed to the rebuilding of the wall, Nehemiah set up a twenty-four-hour-a-day guard. He challenged the people to fight for the protection of the wall-building project. What the Israelites discovered was that their decision to rebuild and fortify the wall provoked an attack from their enemies.

Think about a guard stationed at a castle gate. His primary purpose is to keep unwanted intruders out of the castle, but he is also there to protect something of value that is inside the gate. For Nehemiah it was the capital of his homeland, Jerusalem. For the man desiring to be free from porn, it is his purity. Like Nehemiah, the man who endeavors to truly protect his heart from the immorality of this world will find that the enemy is not going to sit back and say, "Fine. If you want to walk in freedom, go ahead. Build a wall and I'll leave you alone." Instead, he is going to relentlessly attempt to breach your wall and pull you back into sin. Once you have something in your heart as precious as purity, the devil will do anything he can to destroy it.

There are a variety of ways that the enemy will attack your wall. For example, a friend of mine just reached out to me recently to let me know he was getting off a social media platform. Somehow his accountability software was allowing pornographic advertisements to come through on it. He confessed and realized he needed to shut it down completely. Another example might be an unexpected sex scene popping up in a movie or junk email with a link to a porn address. It could also be a message from an old girlfriend or a co-worker who invites you out to coffee. In any of these situations, the way you respond will either protect your wall or allow the enemy to breach it.

Because of the enemy's sly tactics, protecting your boundaries is an ongoing process. Sometimes, a man might discover that his boundaries are overly restrictive and he may decide that he can scale them back a little. However, this can easily end in disaster. For example, I used to have a shopping app on my phone that I occasionally used. It somehow dawned on me that I would be able to use it to view movie trailers. What started as a search for Christian movies ended up with me watching a movie trailer that I knew would be completely sensual. I immediately felt convicted and deleted the app from my phone. I knew that if I did not repair the breach in the wall, the devil would tempt me again and the door could be opened to more sexual content. My failure showed me how important my wall of protection was.

Technology is constantly changing so protecting your wall is an evolving battle and requires vigilance. It is wiser to have overly restrictive boundaries, and adjust as needed, than to allow loose boundaries that set you up for a fall.

PRINCIPLE #5:

Nehemiah Dedicated the Wall to the Lord

At the dedication of the wall of Jerusalem, the Levites were sought out from where they lived and were brought to Jerusalem to celebrate joyfully the dedication with songs of thanksgiving and with the music of cymbals, harps and lyres. (**Nehemiah 12:27 NIV**)

You can imagine the joy in the Israelite community when the final brick was laid and the work ended. They had persevered through the relentless attacks of their enemies and miraculously succeeded in building the wall in fifty-two days. After the project was complete, Nehemiah did something that might seem unrelated to our discussion in this chapter, but it is very much an integral part of this process: He held a large celebration to dedicate the wall to God.

What we have mostly talked about up to this point is the practical nuts-and-bolts aspect of protecting ourselves from ungodly influences. But ultimately, this entire process needs to be implemented in conjunction with the Lord. After all, the primary purpose is to have a vibrant relationship with Him. You are not the only one concerned about your purity. God Himself is also on your side, and that is an amazing advantage because He can see every detail of your life. He knows where things will go if they are left unchecked. Ultimately, the Holy Spirit is the best protection from sexual sin. Everything else we have discussed—when done in conjunction with Him—can provide solid protection. Nevertheless, the practical boundaries will fail without the Protector. He will give you wisdom and discernment if you ask Him because this is His will for your life. As Paul told the Thessalonians: "This is the will of God, your sanctification: that you should abstain from sexual immorality."[5]

As you walk through this process of building and fortifying your wall of protection, take a moment to dedicate your wall to God. Thank Him for bringing you to a point in your life that you care enough about your purity to work through this process. Ask Him for His wisdom and insight on how to navigate your personal wall-building project to make it the most effective it can be. We have a beautiful promise in James 1:5, "If any of you lacks wisdom, let him ask of God, who gives to all liberally and without reproach, and it will be given to him." If there is any area of your wall-building plan that is unclear, just ask the Lord and He will show you what to do.

WHEN A WALL IS NOT ENOUGH

What do you do if you find yourself in a place where this wall-building process is not enough to maintain freedom? Sometimes, a man does not do as much as he should to eliminate porn access. In his heart, there is such a strong pull toward it that he is constantly finding a way around the defense system that he has implemented. Part of this process is not only about developing healthy boundaries, it is also a test of a man's sincerity in getting free. An inability or unwillingness to build a strong wall of protection is a sign that something deeper is needed.

When I am working with a man who fits this description, I will suggest he enter the Pure Life Ministries residential program. If you find that there is no real progress by the time you get to this point in the process, do not give up or grow discouraged. Instead, consider reaching out to Pure Life to see what options are available. I have told many men, "What is the harm in a phone call? Why not just reach out and see what they have to say?" It was an initial phone call that the Lord used to convince me that I needed to be there. In the end, it all comes down to a man's heart. If he is serious about doing business with God, I can guarantee that He will enlist Heaven to fight alongside him. But if he really just wants his sin, not even the Lord Himself will be able to pry his hands off it.

In the next chapter, we will discuss the power that comes from joining with other men to fight in the battle with us. Like Nehemiah, we do not need to guard our walls by ourselves. Having others in our lives to fight alongside us is a great encouragement and reinforcement for our freedom.

CHAPTER 13

Control:// build-a-wall

PRAYER POINTS

- Pray that the modern church will return to the pursuit of true holiness

- Pray for protection over those in your life who are most vulnerable to the enemy's attacks (including yourself)

- Pray for wisdom and insight from the Holy Spirit to direct you (and your family if applicable) to have a strong wall of defense against the allurements and temptations of the world system

DISCUSSION QUESTIONS

1. What about Nehemiah's wall-building story do you find the most encouraging? What do you find the most challenging?

2. Describe the lifestyle of a man who does not prioritize his wall of protection. What would be different between him and a man who genuinely seeks to implement a strong wall around him and his family?

3. What Scriptures can you find that confirm the idea that God desires to come alongside you and help you overcome the world's pull in your life?

4. What does this chapter reveal about a guard's responsibility to not only keep unwanted influences out, but also to keep desirable things safe within the walls? What are those things that a man should desire to protect and how should that motivate him into action?

5. React to the following quote in the chapter: "While some might think that a life with such strict boundaries is not true freedom, I contend that the Bible is a book of boundaries. When we live within those boundaries, we are truly free."

PERSONAL APPLICATION QUESTIONS

1. What specific boundaries do you need to work on in your life? Which areas can you see the greatest opportunity for the enemy to tempt you into compromise?

2. Go through the assessment included in Principle Two. Take the time to journal your answers as well as have a conversation with a trusted mentor and/ or spouse about what you need to change.

3. Do you find yourself resisting the concept of limiting or ridding certain pleasures in your life for the sake of a deeper walk with God? How can you take steps to tackle those areas through prayer and practical action?

14

Insert:// join-forces

WHEN YOU THINK ABOUT THE New Testament, one of the most significant people that comes to mind is the Apostle Paul. He is not only responsible for writing at least thirteen books of the New Testament, but he also became an apostle through a supernatural vision of Christ and worked tirelessly to spread the Gospel throughout the regions surrounding Israel. To say that Paul was a prominent figure in the history of Christianity would be a huge understatement. However, there is a lesser-known man who was very significant in his life, and his name was Barnabas.

When Paul first came to Christ, he was known as Saul, a zealous Pharisee and persecutor of the church. He was responsible for the imprisonment and even murder of many Christians. Needless to say, when word got out that Saul had gotten saved and was preaching the Gospel, it raised many red flags for the church leadership. Acts 9 tells us the story of how Barnabas came alongside Paul and was responsible for his acceptance into the Christian community:

And when Saul had come to Jerusalem, he tried to join the disciples; but they were all afraid of him, and did not believe that he was a disciple. But Barnabas took him and brought him to the apostles. And he declared to them how he had seen the Lord on the road, and that He had spoken to him, and how he had preached boldly at Damascus in the name of Jesus. (**Acts 9:26-27**)

Barnabas' name means "son of encouragement."[1] He became one of Paul's traveling companions and worked closely with him in the ministry. While there is no biblical evidence that Paul and Barnabas ever kept each other accountable for their purity, their relationship provides a powerful illustration of what it means for two men to come alongside each other and follow Jesus together. Paul was not a "one man show" as some might imagine. As a single man with deeply held convictions about sexual purity, one can only assume that he kept this area of his life in check and walked in transparency with men like Barnabas. As the Bible describes the process of one man sharpening another like iron sharpening iron[2], I think it is safe to say that Paul would not have become the man he did without the influence of Barnabas in his life.

I have personally seen the incredible advantage of having "sons of encouragement" in my life. In fact, I am certain I would not be the man I am today without their influence. This chapter will explain the crucial importance of having men of God in our lives who can keep us accountable. For me, this is a non-negotiable spiritual discipline.

BEING REAL WITH PEOPLE AROUND YOU

Shortly after I graduated from Pure Life Ministries, I was in a season of real struggle. While I did not have any easy access to view porn, I had the thought that if my wife logged me into her laptop for a moment—and she was in another room—I could quickly search for nude pictures and just delete the history. It was a temptation I tried hard to fight off, but I made the mistake of trying to battle on my own. Unfortunately, I allowed the thought to run around in my mind for a couple of days instead of bringing it into the light.

One night, I asked my wife to sign me into her laptop. When she did, she stepped away briefly. With that short window of temptation, I gave in. I probably saw an image or two for less than two seconds before I clicked out, but even that brief exposure deeply convicted me. I had a decision to make. Was I going to confess to my wife, or was I going to keep it a secret?

Initially, I thought I could fix the problem without having to tell her. I could casually suggest that I had noticed that our computer did not have accountability software, and that even though I rarely used it, maybe it would be better to have it on the laptop…just in case. My wife probably would not have thought much of it. I could have "covered up my tracks" and no one would get hurt in the process. Dealing with it that way, I would be able to avoid breaking my wife's trust and would not have had to admit that I was still susceptible to looking at porn.

Thankfully, the Holy Spirit has kept me on a short leash, so to speak, ever since my initial repentance. He will not let me have peace when I try to cover things up anymore. I knew that God was telling me that I needed to share what happened. So, I confessed, and she advised me to meet with our pastor. After I told him what I had done and we prayed together, I did the only thing I could do: dust off my feet and keep walking. But I did not stop there. I also installed a content blocker on that computer so that even if I was on it alone, I would not have the temptation to get into porn. If I had kept everything in the dark, I can only imagine where it could have taken me and the many regrets I might have faced from it.

This event was a significant spiritual test I experienced at the beginning of my journey into freedom. It was the first of many difficult conversations I have had over the years with accountability partners. It is never easy to be open about sinful thoughts or actions. However, 1 John 1:7 tells us, "If we walk in the light as He is in the light, we have fellowship with one another, and the blood of Jesus Christ His Son cleanses us from all sin." Walking in the light is a continual process, and we never graduate from the need to live in transparency. My openness and honesty with my wife and others have not only created a safety net for me but have also reestablished my trust.

That being said, my wife is not the person that I tell everything to all the time. I do not believe a wife should be that person, because it unnecessarily reinforces her fears and insecurities. That is why I have men in my life that I can fully bare my soul to, who hold my feet to the fire. I am so grateful to the Lord that I learned that lesson early on, because it has insulated me from going back into sexual sin all these years.

THE ROLE OF ACCOUNTABILITY

Accountability is a buzzword in addiction recovery circles, which is understandable because the man who wants to live in freedom needs others with him on the journey. Some men want to be lone rangers and handle everything by themselves, missing the fact that the Lord has given us other brothers to walk alongside us. We can easily deceive ourselves, so having someone else's insight is very valuable. However, accountability is something that needs to be clearly defined. Patrick Morley explains it this way:

> "Accountability doesn't evolve naturally in a relationship; it results from a purposed decision to live our lives in a 'goldfish bowl' before a few men we learn to trust. Not only does accountability give someone permission to ask us hard questions, but asking those hard questions forms the basis for the relationship. Sometimes things can get sticky, but the friendship side of the relationship cannot be allowed to mute the accountability role."[3]

I learned through experience that accountability is not limited to confessing sin to another man. Certainly, confession is part of the process, but who you are confessing to and what they do with that confession makes all the difference in an accountability relationship. Here are four principles to keep in mind when it comes to accountability.

PRINCIPLE #1:

True Accountability Includes
Total Transparency

Accountability relationships require intentional effort from everyone involved to pursue transparency. The challenge of opening up to someone else is the temptation to only share part of what is actually going on inside. Our flesh will naturally resist and avoid exposing our hearts to other men. Sometimes in a conversation, we might be tempted to downplay the severity of something we did: "Well, I went down the rabbit hole on social media, but didn't actually look at porn." We might try to cover it up: "I had a decent week. It could've been better, but I'm pressing forward." It is this internal self-protection that causes us to only say enough so we feel like we are being honest without really getting down to the truth of our inside world. However, it is those deeper-level, gut-wrenching, painful conversations that cause the greatest breakthroughs. Essentially, accountability is only truly effective when you are talking about the things *that you do not want to talk about*.

Any man who has attempted to live a life of transparency has found that everything inside of him will resist it. The moment he gives in to temptation, the thought immediately comes, "No one has to find out about this." Then shame will keep him from reaching out to people he knows will pray for him. Or maybe he will justify himself, "They are probably busy, and I don't want to disappoint them again." Of course, we should never lose sight of the fact that the enemy is very much a part of the battle. He knows if he can keep us from being totally transparent, then he can keep a hook in our hearts and use it to lure us back into sin.

Sitting down with a man of God and being completely honest with him is a powerful part of overcoming. When you open your heart and give a trusted partner the uncensored version of what you are dealing with, it is like the power of that temptation is broken and the door is slammed shut. Temptation builds, like a balloon slowly filling with air; it seems like it will pop if you do not give into it. Confession is like letting the air out of the balloon. The pressure just dissipates when you bring darkness into the light.

While accountability often involves just one other man in your life, having a small group of men come together to practice transparency can also be an effective way to establish these relationships. I have experienced accountability one-on-one, with a small group of three men as well as a larger group from our church. Any of these options can work as long as total transparency is practiced. If a larger group causes you to restrain from being honest, make sure you have at least one man that you tell everything to.

As you are considering setting up an accountability system, commitment to confidentiality is essential. You need to connect with men who would never share the details of your personal life with others. That type of trust takes time to be established but should be communicated early in the accountability relationship. This mutual confidentiality becomes even more important when your accountability system includes a group of men.

It takes time for trust to be built in a group, which can make it difficult for guys to be fully transparent. I tell the men I meet with, "Everything that is shared here stays between us. Obviously, if there is something that needs to be dealt with legally or within your marriage, we will walk through it together. But nothing that is shared here should ever be shared outside of our group." You want to find men that you can trust and will fight for you. There also needs to be a mutual agreement to share the complete truth. Part of that commitment means that if you ever downplay or minimize something, you go back and confess it to your brothers. Only a commitment to total transparency and truthfulness will build lasting freedom through accountability.

PRINCIPLE #2:

An Accountability Partner Needs to Be Spiritually Mature

In Bible college, I became close friends with a roommate who also struggled with porn. We decided to do what we considered to be spiritually wise and become accountability partners. Our accountability system worked something like this: I would be tempted to look at pornography. Sometimes I might reach out to him before I gave in, but more often I would sin, feel guilty, call him and confess. He would pray with me and would encourage me to keep pressing on. Later, the same conversation would repeat itself, except the shoe would be on the other foot, and it would be me praying for him after his confession. While I am certain that we were both sincerely trying to help each other, the reality is that, even after an extended season, we were both still in bondage.

Looking back, I realized that I was only using our accountability as a way to appease my guilt. Getting our sin out in the open became more of a means to pacify the pain than to pull each other out of sin. This unhealthy situation continued after I got married, helping to convince me that I did not need to share my struggles with my wife. Again, our intentions were good. We really believed that we were helping each other, and I suppose it was better than remaining silent. However, it was a faulty accountability system.

When two people discover that they share the same struggles, it only makes sense to be accountable to each other. But as time goes on, they will discover that the very system intended to bring freedom actually helps keep them in chains. Having someone to confess to diminishes the feeling of guilt about ongoing sin, but the system becomes little better than an unrepentant sinner confessing to a priest. Confession may seem like a spiritual action, but it is not enough to keep us from our sin.

Another accountability structure that was unsuccessful for me was a Christian twelve-step program. After a time of worship and study, we would break into groups and discuss our lives on a deeper level. This particular group made a habit of confessing sin to one another on a weekly basis. I got into a cycle where I would get high or drunk before I went, confess to the group and leave the meeting feeling better about myself. But there was no call to repentance and no one to keep me accountable for my sin. In fact, as I was sinning, I would tell myself, "I'll just tell the group this week so that it's out there."

These scenarios taught me the importance of being careful about my motives when it comes to accountability. You need to find a man or group of men with a real walk with God who are willing to truly keep you accountable. That means asking the hard questions, and at times, being willing to lovingly confront you. You need someone who is going to help pull you out of sin and keep you from going back. Asking the Lord to find the right man for your situation is so crucial because this is a vital area of continuing to walk in freedom.

PRINCIPLE #3:

Accountability Cannot Replace the Holy Spirit

Another potential flaw of an accountability system is looking to other people as a source of help and strength rather than the Holy Spirit. Accountability done right should push you toward the Lord and into greater dependence on Him. It should cause you to grow in your faith and strengthen your relationship with Jesus. You have a problem if it causes you to put your trust in a person. You need to learn to continually depend on the Lord for help. After all, your accountability partner cannot be with you at every moment of every day. But the Holy Spirit will, and He has the power to help you maintain purity.

This is why you need godly men in your life who will not just help you to stay away from porn but will point you to the cross. They will be concerned about the quality of your walk with God and teach you how to rely on the Holy Spirit. As Paul said, "Walk in the Spirit, and you shall not fulfill the lust of the flesh."[4] Because porn is the epitome of the lust of the flesh, learning to walk in the Spirit is a key factor in your freedom. Any form of accountability you have must cause you to lean on the Holy Spirit more than any man.

Taking the time to examine your accountability relationships is wise. After a meeting or phone conversation, ask the question, "Did that cause me to want to press into the Lord deeper? Or was it more of a lifeless exercise?" You need men who deeply care about your spiritual life, not just your freedom from pornography.

PRINCIPLE #4:

Accountability is Broader Than Sexual Purity

In the context of this book, most will think about sexual purity as the sole purpose for having an accountability partner. But my personal experience has led me to believe that every Christian man needs accountability in his life. While purity is an obvious area of concern for most men, there are many other areas of a man's life that are also important.*** These include topics like marriage, parenting, business dealings, finances and integrity. While it is not possible to get into deep discussions about all these areas in one accountability meeting, it is important to tackle various aspects of your life as you get together.

I recently started a men's accountability breakfast. I usually give the men one or two pre-planned questions and then ask them to share about their lives: the good, the bad and the ugly. Having questions prepared and written down helps to guide the discussion and acts as an effective icebreaker. After all, for many men, it is easier to read a question off a paper than to ask tough questions directly. However, the closer that you grow in your relationship, the more layers you will uncover that go deeper than general questions. In the past, I have created a personal list of questions for my accountability partners that is specific to my own battles and spiritual goals. The point is to have a plan when you meet for accountability so that you are addressing different areas of your life that need to be talked about beyond purity.

THE PROTECTION OF TRUE FELLOWSHIP

The closest biblical concept to true accountability is the Greek word *koinonia*. It is translated as *fellowship*, but as one source explains, "No single English word adequately translates its meaning…this is not just a fellowship with other people, for it expresses at the deepest level spiritual fellowship that is 'in Christ.'"[5] For those who have never developed this kind of deep heart-connection with another brother in the Lord, it can be

---

***See Appendix D for a list of accountability questions covering multiple aspects of a man's life

difficult to understand its value. However, once you step into that realm of true accountability, it can be a game changer in your journey of freedom. As Dietrich Bonhoeffer once explained:

> "A man who confesses his sins in the presence of a brother knows that he is no longer alone with himself; he experiences the presence of God in the reality of the other person. As long as I am by myself in the confession of my sins, everything remains in the clear, but in the presence of a brother, the sin has to be brought into the light."[6]

I have a couple of men in my life with whom I have established this kind of deep, intimate relationship. We can share everything with one another and because we know each other so well, the wisdom we can provide each other is extremely valuable. Koinonia is a rich source of blessing to any man who pursues it.

James 5:16 states, "Confess your trespasses to one another, and pray for one another, that you may be healed." To have at least one man in your life that you can be gut-wrenchingly honest with is a safeguard that men cannot disregard. I hate to think what my life might be like today if I did not have men in my life who have held me accountable and have strengthened me with their prayers and encouragement. What if I never had men to talk about temptation or confess sin to? How easy it would have been to go back into my sin.

A proper response to this step in the process is to begin praying for God to lead you to that man or men who can become a source of true accountability in your life. Ask Him to bring you a "son of encouragement" like Barnabas. If you already have a system in place, consider bringing these ideas to your accountability relationship to increase its effectiveness. Because of my personal experience with the power of true accountability, I believe this is an essential spiritual discipline for every Christian man. It helps to propel us into spiritual maturity in a way that does not happen individually.

In the next chapter, I want to dispel some common misconceptions that men have about walking in freedom that I hope will be a great encouragement on your journey.

CHAPTER 14

Insert:// join-forces

PRAYER POINTS

- Pray that men in your social circle would be convinced of their need for true transparency and accountability and that these types of healthy relationships would be formed in their lives

- Pray that men in the Body of Christ would experience a genuine revival and a return to their spiritual roles as men of God

- Pray that the Lord will provide you with a strong man/ group of men that you can build a deep koinonia relationship with

DISCUSSION QUESTIONS

1. What approach do most churches take with accountability from your perspective? How effective has this been in your experience?

2. How does the definition of koinonia differ from the average friendships that a man in church might have?

3. Patrick Morley wrote, "Accountability doesn't evolve naturally in a relationship; it results from a purposed decision to live our lives in a 'goldfish bowl' before a few men we learn to trust." What are practical ways that men can intentionally forge these relationships?

4. Why do many men have a difficult time being totally transparent with others? What fears keep them from experiencing this full transparency?

5. What other areas of a man's life might accountability have a profound impact on?

PERSONAL APPLICATION QUESTIONS

1. Are you currently being accountable to another man/ men in your life? What is the depth of true transparency you are experiencing in that relationship?

2. What steps can you take to either establish or strengthen an accountability relationship in your life?

3. Do you have concerns about allowing another man into your inner world? What are those obstacles you are facing and how can you overcome them?

15

Shift:// set-realistic-expectations

I WAS COUNSELING SOMEONE RECENTLY and we were discussing freedom from sexual sin. I mentioned that those who have been set free from bondage to porn can still experience seasons when lust is a challenge. He asked me a pointed question: "If a man can still struggle with lust, how do you know they are truly free?" I admitted to him that this is a question I still wrestle with at times. How does the Bible define freedom and how much leeway can we give ourselves in our fight against sexual sin? Does purity mean that we win one hundred percent of the battles in thought and action? Unfortunately, the Scriptures do not answer those questions as clearly as most men would like. I can admit that I was sorely disappointed with the fact that my sinful flesh had not changed even after deleting pornography from my life. However, I have learned some things along the way that have been encouraging on my journey. Here are five principles about what a life of freedom looks like on a practical basis.

PRINCIPLE #1:

Temptation Does Not Equal Sin

Temptation and sin are not the same. The purpose of every temptation is to lead us into sin but experiencing it does not mean that we have crossed that line. This is a needed truth for the man who endeavors to walk in freedom because he will quickly discover that deleting porn from his life does not eliminate temptation.

Hebrews 4:15 tells us that Jesus "was in all points tempted as we are, yet without sin." Our Savior lived a completely sinless life. If He had sinned even one time, it would have ruined our chances at salvation because He would no longer have been the perfect, sacrificial Lamb. Yet this passage tells us that Jesus was tempted in every way that we are. That reveals something important about our own battle with sin: The fact that Jesus experienced temptation and yet did not sin means that our propensity to be tempted sexually is not an indicator that we are giving into sin.

This passage in Hebrews implies that Jesus was tempted sexually. Think about it. He was fully man, just like you and I, which means He had a sex drive. That may be an uncomfortable thought in a world in which sex can be seen as dirty and shameful, but it is true. Jesus lived thirty-three years on this earth. I am sure that He encountered beautiful women in His day. We know that He came into contact with some who were promiscuous, such as the woman caught in adultery[1] and the woman who anointed His feet with tears.[2] But the Son of God had to learn to bring His sexual desires under the control of the Holy Spirit just like we do. Because He succeeded, He set an example for us of complete sexual purity. How encouraging it is that Jesus took on a human body with the same reproductive system that we have and, despite temptation, never sinned.

Temptation leaves some men with feelings of guilt and shame. I have had men confide to me that they were plagued with sexual dreams even after getting free from pornography. "I feel so dirty when that happens," they lament. "Do I need to repent even though I had no choice in the matter?" I tell them, "You need to bring it to the Lord and ask for cleansing, and don't allow the enemy to overrun you with feelings of guilt and condemnation. You can't control your thinking when you're asleep. Most likely they're part of the consequences of your past life of giving over to sexualized thinking. They'll probably become less common the further you distance yourself from porn. I would encourage you to read the Word of God right before you go to sleep to help keep your mind on the Lord. Ask the Holy Spirit to protect your mind while you're asleep. It's a great way to bring Him into the situation."

Temptation is not sinful, but giving over to it is. Noticing an attractive woman is also not sinful; it is the second lustful glance that causes you to cross the line. Likewise, just having a sexual thought is not necessarily sinful because the enemy is able to plant tempting thoughts into our minds. However, we need to be honest with ourselves that we have given the devil plenty of ammunition from the pornographic images we have filled our minds with. Nevertheless, allowing a sexual thought to linger rather than taking it captive and making it obedient to Christ[3] causes us to cross the line into sin.

In his book, *At the Altar of Sexual Idolatry*, Steve Gallagher defines two types of lust: proactive and reactive. Proactive lust is when we intentionally use our minds to focus on lustful thoughts and reactive lust occurs when we respond to a temptation sinfully. Both forms of lust begin with a temptation in the mind and can be prevented from crossing into sin if it is dealt with properly and immediately. Living in a fallen world, temptation is inescapable. However, we can choose to react the way that Jesus modeled: being tempted, yet without sin.

PRINCIPLE #2:

Freedom is Not Perfection

Someone might say, "It's not temptation that I'm concerned about. I know that I am still crossing the line sometimes. I am taking the second, third, and fourth glances and even allow my mind to fantasize. What about me?" Some men live in a constant state of guilt and doubt about their spiritual condition because they are not victorious in every battle they face.

I want to emphasize that I have not personally mastered a completely lust-free life. At times, I still battle with my thought life and I need to continually be aware of where my eyes wander. Do I win 100% of the time? No. Sometimes, I fail and need to repent. But I do see growth and my hope is still in the cross. Often, people ask me about the difference between my life before and after Pure Life Ministries. I answer this way. "I still have issues with lust, but it no longer controls my mind. I have learned how to fight, and I win far more battles than I lose."

However, I do not want to get too cocky about my life of freedom, nor develop the attitude of some men: "Take it easy. Why are you making such a big deal about looking at some woman? Think of how far you've come. At least you aren't given over to pornography and sexual sin anymore!" While it is true that I am extremely grateful I am not where I once was, I refuse to allow myself to feel comfortable with lust in my life. I try to take Jesus' words to heart that even internal thoughts are the same as acting out externally.[4] Any time we fall short of His standard—even when it is only on the inside—we need to learn to immediately take it to the Lord and repent. And once we have repented, we just keep moving forward.

I have been through seasons in which I thought the battle was over. I have experienced lengthy periods when lust seemed to be the farthest thing from my mind. Inevitably, something would change, and I would find myself back in the battle. There are seasons of reprieve and seasons to fight. No matter what season I am in, however, my goal is always complete purity in word, thought and action. When I do fall short, I refuse to allow discouragement to keep me down; I get right back into the fight. The promise of 1 John 1:9 is a beautiful and potent passage of Scripture: "If we confess our sins, He is faithful and just to forgive us our sins and to cleanse us from all unrighteousness." When used in its proper context, it is one of the most precious promises the Lord gives to His children. His grace and mercy are available for any man who truly repents.

Freedom from pornography is not the absence of temptation; it only means that you have learned to fight. Being free from lust does not mean that you will never deal with it again. It all comes down to whether or not you are truly fighting. If you are actively resisting your flesh and sinful tendencies, then you will continue to press on even if you have occasional setbacks.

This should be a liberating truth to the man who is sincerely pressing into the Lord and walking in repentance. He will be able to take a deep breath, realize his hope is in the Lord, and continue on the journey. The man who wants to live without conviction about his sin might take this principle and use it for selfish purposes, but he is only deceiving himself. It really comes down to the motive of one's heart.

PRINCIPLE #3:

Falling Does Not Mean You've Lost All Progress

A man might say, "It's not just a fleeting thought I'm battling with. I actually fell back into pornography. What do *I* do?" I want to be very intentional on how I address this concept because in no way do I want to make people feel that they are free to continue in sin. However, you might ask the question, "What if I am walking in true freedom and I fall into pornography in a moment of weakness?" Of course, this can happen. You should not live with the expectation that going back to porn is inevitable. However, if you do, the way that you respond can determine how quickly you get back on your feet spiritually.

There have been multiple occasions over the years where I have drifted into sinful territory on the internet in a moment of weakness. I had to confess, bring it into the light and tighten the grip on my boundaries. Even with the strong wall of protection I have built for myself, there have been times when there is a breach, and temptation begins to draw me back down that path. So, when I tell people I have been free from porn for over a decade, I do not mean that I have not thought, heard or seen anything sexual during that period. However, those instances have been short in duration, rare in occurrence and mild in depth. They have been brought into the light quickly, dealt with severely and put behind me immediately. This is a completely different lifestyle than when I was frequently, deeply, consistently going from one pornographic experience to another.

The temptation for a man who slips or even falls is to feel like he is back at square one. It feels like he has totally blown his purity. The enemy is quick to whisper in his ear: "See, you haven't changed at all. You're the same person. You aren't free and never will be. God hasn't done anything in your life." Many feel that an event like this would completely destroy their progress, as if they would have to start back from the beginning.

While working with men who are learning to walk in purity, often at the beginning of their journey, they will confess to me that they gave in during a moment of weakness. If they are truly repentant, I tell them, "Don't let the devil use condemnation to beat you up and discourage you. If you have done business with God, receive His forgiveness, and *keep walking forward!*" What often happens is that men allow the devil to gain a foothold. He will whisper to them, "Well, you've given into your sin. You might as well go do it again. You have to go to God for forgiveness for this anyhow; you might as well enjoy your sin a little while longer. You can always repent later." If you realize that this is one of his tactics, you can guard your heart from being tempted again. Will you have bad moments? Of course. The important thing is that you do not let those moments turn into days, weeks or even months.

I heard an illustration once from Sy Rogers that I have never forgotten regarding sexual sin. He said something along these lines, "Imagine you are racing around a track on a bicycle, but halfway through the race, you fall over. Do you automatically get transported back to the starting line to restart the race? No! You simply pick up where you fell, dust your feet off, get back on the bike and keep going."[5] This advice is liberating for the sincere man who is pursuing freedom yet gives into temptation in a moment of weakness. Obviously, this concept does not apply to the man who gives into sin continually. If that is your lifestyle, you need to ask yourself the question, "Am I even in the race or am I just sitting at the starting line?"

Giving into temptation does not eliminate your progress. Maybe you will never fall outwardly again; I hope that is true. However, you will certainly have to fight inwardly. There will be lustful thoughts to battle, covetousness that creeps into your heart and an imagination that you will have to learn to control. Unless you live in a cave somewhere, you will be around people who are physically attractive which can arouse sexual desire within you. You may be sitting in the waiting room at a doctor's office and notice a trashy magazine. Or perhaps an ad will pop-up while you are checking your email. The temptations are everywhere. So, like it or not, your decision to walk in purity just enlisted you into a spiritual battle. There is no shortcut to purity. It requires you to fight one day at a time, one battle at a time, if you want to maintain the freedom that you desperately seek.

I want to emphasize that because of Jesus and the power of the cross, if you are a born again believer, you do not *have* to give into lust. In fact, Jude 1:24 declares that God "is able to keep you from stumbling." With His help, you can resist temptation and live in purity. But even if you do succumb to sin, you "have an Advocate with the Father, Jesus Christ the righteous."[6]

PRINCIPLE #4:

When Pursuing Freedom, Time is On Your Side

While the old adage, "Time heals all wounds" is misleading, it is true that time can certainly be on your side when it comes to freedom from sexual sin. The reason this is true is that the longer you abstain from pornography, the easier it gets to stay away from it. In the beginning of deleting porn from your life, you might feel that the road is just too long. Freedom seems light years away, and you find it difficult to believe that you will ever become free. However, something helpful occurs as you put distance between you and your sin day by day, week by week, month by month and year by year. You are increasing the distance between the pornographic images and your memory.

While it is true that many of those images will stay with you for a long time, the longer you are removed from them, the fuzzier they become in your mind. After several years, I am now only able to remember the scenes that really had a marked impression on my mind. There are thousands of images and movies that have completely vanished. I have also found that the longer I am removed from porn, the more control I have over those memories when they do occur. In the beginning stages of the battle, there were many images that remained pretty vivid. Now, I would have to make an intentional effort to remember them. Keep fighting, it does get easier!

PRINCIPLE #5:

Repentance is Both an Event and a Process

I was part of a question-and-answer panel at a men's meeting for sexual sin recently. A young man asked a very insightful question about Psalm 51. He inquired, "David prayed that God would restore the joy of his salvation. At what specific point in David's process did that happen, since we are not told in Scripture?" As I pondered his question, the Lord reminded me of something I heard years ago. When we think about sexual sin, we often have an event-based mindset. We think, "If I respond to an altar call or do some other specific action, then repentance will happen in that moment." However, the reality is that repentance is more complicated than that. God is not only concerned about events in our lives, but He also uses processes to change us.

For instance, consider the birth of a baby. The day that child comes into the world is an event, but it is also the culmination of a nine-month process. So, if you ask if a birth is an event or a process, the answer is "Yes." Repentance is very similar. While the event can be a man's response to the conviction of the Holy Spirit, it is really the beginning of a process that typically takes time, especially when it involves overcoming years of sexual addiction. When I reflect on my own repentance, although I did have a significant breakthrough season that propelled me forward, it occurred through a long and sometimes painful process.

This is why men who want to get free from porn should not place all their expectancy on a single prayer, a call to response or any other "event." While these things are a valuable part of the process, in and of themselves, they are usually only one piece of an intricate puzzle. Men often want God to do an instant miracle so that they do not have to go through the messy and painful work involved in the process of repentance. The Lord will use the process to build something into your character that will help you go the distance in your freedom. So, if you are frustrated that you did not receive some massive breakthrough when you exposed your sin, uttered a prayer or responded to an altar call, do not be discouraged. If you truly desire to please the Lord, He will do the work of repentance that is needed.

As you are coming toward the end of your journey through *Delete*, I think it is healthy to understand what to expect on this side of freedom. Being free from porn may not look exactly like what you expect. I do not know if that will encourage or discourage you but having realistic expectations is important. As we have seen, a life of freedom does not mean that there is no struggle, temptation or setbacks. Instead, it is a life of learning to fight through the struggles, resist the temptations and persevere through the setbacks. Keep focused on the long-term plan. The walk of freedom is a marathon, not a sprint.

In the final chapter, we are going to talk about what it looks like to use your freedom to make an impact in the world around you for Jesus.

CHAPTER 15

Shift:// set-realistic-expectations

PRAYER POINTS

- Pray that God will help other men who have read or will read *Delete* to go the distance in their journey into freedom, allowing the Lord to accomplish His will in their lives

- Pray that the Lord will give you the proper perspective on what this journey is going to look like as well as a sincere desire to spiritually fight

- Pray for other men in your life who might be going through struggles of any kind, that the Lord will give them victory in their battle

DISCUSSION QUESTIONS

1. What assumptions do most men have about getting free from porn? How has this chapter challenged or affirmed those assumptions?

2. Do you think that most men are hoping for an "easy-button" fix to their porn problem? Why do you think that God does not typically work that way for men battling with sexual sin?

3. Where is the balance between embracing God's grace in failure and abusing His grace to placate the guilt of sin?

4. How does God work in both events and processes? How does that reality apply to a man's freedom journey?

5. Consider the many ways that Jesus must have been tempted as a man. What does His life teach us about the proper way to respond to temptation?

PERSONAL APPLICATION QUESTIONS

1. What are some of your expectations about the future that might be unrealistic or unbiblical?

2. Looking forward, how do you feel about the prospects of permanently deleting porn from your life? (encouraged, fearful, hopeful, unsure, etc.)

3. Do you think that you have treated the grace of God as a license to sin in your life? What checks and balances can you put into place to avoid this going forward?

16

Increase Volume:// become-a-blessing

ENESIS 45 RECORDS A CLIMACTIC moment in the story of Jacob's son, Joseph. He found himself standing face to face with his brothers, who had sold him into slavery and faked his death. Their selfish and wicked actions had set into motion a long series of very painful and traumatic circumstances in Joseph's life. There is no doubt that the temptation to use his power to take revenge on them must have been very real. After all, as the second in command to Pharoah, he could have called for their execution, and it would have been carried out without question.

Perhaps at that moment, as he considered his options, his mind went back to two prophetic dreams he had as a teenager. God had revealed many years before that he would one day rule over his family. Those dreams had become a reality as Joseph's brothers were literally bowing down to him. But could the painful journey he went through really have been the plan of God? It certainly seemed that the evil intentions of man had played a strong part in his initial enslavement and his eventual imprisonment.

If the brothers had known the identity of this Egyptian ruler standing before them, they would have realized just how precarious a situation they were in. Their lives were now at the mercy of the man whose life they had destroyed. Fortunately for those brothers, the man in front of them had a heart that cared more about God's will than taking vengeance. As Joseph shared his speech he must have rehearsed a thousand times, he concluded with this phrase: "You intended to harm me, but God intended it for good to accomplish what is now being done, the saving of many lives."[1]

I cannot think of a better Scripture to explain what has taken place in my own life since I repented of sexual sin. The devil was behind the plot to destroy Joseph's life. In my case, he attempted to destroy my life with drugs and sex. Yet, God intervened in my situation just like He did for Joseph. I, too, can declare that the plan that was meant to destroy my life has now become a tool for God to rescue others out of the dark pit of sin.

As we come to the final chapter of this book, my sincere hope is that you have taken seriously the principles laid out and are allowing the Holy Spirit to lead you into freedom. Once a man has deleted pornography from his life, he now has the exciting opportunity to become a rich blessing in the world around him. When God rescues a man out of darkness, He will look to use his life and testimony to help rescue others out of sin. This is how the Gospel of Jesus Christ is spread throughout the earth.

WHY YOUR FREEDOM MATTERS

I remember the moment when I finally decided to go to Pure Life Ministries. My wife had confronted me about hidden sin that she had discovered, and I finally broke. Yes, I had confessed my sin on the mission field but what followed was eight months of unrepentant darkness. Now I was finally hitting rock bottom. In a moment of sheer desperation, I told her I would do whatever it took to get help, including submitting myself to Pure Life's residential program. It was not long before I made my way down to Dry Ridge, Kentucky.

To be completely transparent, my motivations for going to the program were far from spiritual. I just wanted to get out of the bitter cycle of sin that had consumed my life. I was "sick and tired of being sick and tired," as they say. I longed to be able to experience some semblance of sanity and rest. While keeping my marriage together was a contributing factor in entering the program, even that was for selfish reasons. It was all about me and what I wanted.

Living for self had become my default lifestyle, and it was not without its consequences. I had sown to please my flesh and had reaped destruction.[2] My sin had a devastating effect on those closest to me, especially my wife and family. This was my condition when I set foot on Pure Life's campus on a cool April day in 2011. My life had become a curse to the people around me.

I could never have dreamt at that time what a radical life change I would experience through the program. As I began to fully surrender to Jesus, the repentance process enabled Him to use my life as a channel of His blessing to people around me in ways that I could never have imagined possible. A life that had once been a curse was becoming a blessing. What the enemy had meant for evil, the Lord was turning around for good through an amazing display of His mercy.

Over a decade later, my heart is continually filled with gratitude as I see the Lord using our ministry to impact other people. There are men in several countries who are walking in freedom from sexual sin today because of the work of repentance that the Lord did in my life. Some I have personally counseled while others have taken my advice and sought out biblical counsel for themselves. There are unbelievers who have come into a real relationship with Christ and believers who have experienced spiritual breakthrough in their lives. It humbles me that God has transformed me into a vessel that He can use to minister to others. My boast is completely in the Lord! Only He could take a man who has done the things I have done and make his life have an eternal impact.

When I was in sin, my life resembled a bulldozer, destroying whatever was in its path. Now that the Lord has set me free, my life has become more of a lifeboat, rescuing souls that God brings my way. This is why it matters that *you* get free from the power of sin. It is not just so that you can have a more comfortable life, without the destruction that comes from sexual addiction. Overcoming sexual sin means more than holding your marriage together or continuing in your career or ministry. It is so much bigger than that! God wants to make your life a blessing to other people. He wants to use your life as a trophy of His mercy in order to show a broken world what His love can do for them.

I was recently ministering to the men at Pure Life and declared: "God wants to make you a blessing! He wants to use you in ways that you cannot even imagine right now. Just look at what He has done through my life! All He is looking for is a willing vessel." I know how difficult those words are to receive when you are experiencing the pain and challenges that sexual sin creates. You might be where I was at the beginning of my journey. You may have picked up this book trying to keep your marriage together or to avoid facing further consequences for your sin. Nevertheless, your whole perception would change if you could see the life that God is offering. You only need to surrender to Him.

PEOPLE NEED TO HEAR WHAT GOD HAS DONE

It would be impossible to quantify the number of times that I have had the opportunity to recount my story. I have shared it on street corners, at church altars, in grocery stores, from pulpits, in prison blocks and rehabilitation centers. I have shared it with the young and old, in many settings, from large churches in big cities to very small churches in rural areas. My story has been translated into Spanish, Portuguese, Dutch and Macedonian, and been shared in numerous countries throughout the world. What is incredible to me is how the Lord has used it to encourage, convict, inspire and amaze those who hear it.

Hearing my testimony has emboldened many men to be transparent about their own struggles with pornography. I should mention that I do not believe it was God's will for me to go through my years of sexual sin. My story is filled with my selfish, sinful choices that hurt my relationship with God and people I dearly love. But, just as He did with Joseph, I am firmly convinced that He is able to use painful and terrible stories such as mine to rescue others.

If God has set you free and kept you free, your testimony is desperately needed in the church today. If the statistics we discussed in the first chapter are even remotely accurate, at least half of professing Christian men are involved with pornography. That means that half the men sitting in your church are into porn and probably desperate to delete it from their lives. You may have been one of them, but now the Lord has given you a fresh chance to live in freedom. Is it not possible, even probable, that you could connect with at least one other man and share the hope that God has given you?

Imagine if every man in the church who has been set free from porn made it their personal mission to pray for other men in bondage and seek to share their testimony with them. The message that Jesus has the power to set men free from sexual sin would spread throughout the Body of Christ exponentially. More men would be emboldened to speak freely about their struggles, and we would see many more plucked out of the grip of the enemy! You and I have the opportunity to be a part of that process, and it can all happen as we endeavor to share our story with others.

It is not just other men in church who need to know your story. What about men in your extended family, such as your son, grandson or nephew? How about your unsaved co-worker who is hopelessly lost in sin and has no idea that there is a Savior who can save him and set him free? This world needs to see what it looks like for a man of God to walk in purity, integrity, holiness and the power of the Holy Spirit. The Lord wants to make each of us that kind of man.

HOW REPENTANCE IMPACTS OTHERS

In Psalm 51:13, David prayed the following words about the effect his repentance would have on other people: "Then I will teach transgressors Your ways, and sinners shall be converted to You." As David was working through his process, he told the Lord that if He would cleanse, forgive and restore him, he would teach sinners His ways. The result would be that they too would come into a right relationship with Him. This part of his psalm might seem unrelated to what he had written before. The majority of his prayer was all about his sin and his relationship with God. David understood that he could not make an impact on the lives of others while he was in ongoing sin. Now that he was coming into freedom, he wanted the Lord to use him to help rescue others.

This passage reveals that the person who truly repents will not only find freedom for himself but can also be involved in helping others get free. As the sin diminishes in a man's life, so too will his selfish preoccupation with his own desires. It will not be long before the Lord will begin to burden him with the needs of others. As that happens, he will find that his temptations to sin will be less frequent and less intense. Also, as previously mentioned, there is a spiritual power in showing mercy to others. It has a transformative element to it that shifts the direction of our hearts from receiving selfishly to giving mercifully. With that in mind, below are some practical ways that you can use the freedom God has given you to bless others.

As a disclaimer, I would encourage every man to include a trusted spiritual leader in the process of choosing which of these to implement. This is because some of them require a greater measure of spiritual maturity than others. Finding practical ways to meet needs in the lives of others can be done by any man reading these words. However, starting a Bible study or entering a mentoring relationship with a man struggling with porn will require a greater measure of maturity and a substantial period of freedom. A mature spiritual leader will help you navigate the timing and wisdom of implementing these ideas.

Meet Simple Needs

Simple acts of kindness done in Jesus' name might not sound very impactful, but doing something tangible as an act of love for others is an effective way to start a spiritual conversation. Most people are stunned when someone blesses them without expecting anything in return. This will lead them to ask "Why?" That question opens the door to explain the love of God and the hope of the Gospel. Meeting needs can be as simple as paying for someone's meal at a restaurant, handing out a gift card at a grocery store or mowing the lawn for an elderly neighbor. Every time you serve another person, your self-life that has been fertile ground for sexual sin is diminished. Not only that, but it will train you to become more cognizant of the needs of people around you and help to develop the heart of a servant inside you.

Serve in Your Local Church or Ministry

Typically, churches seek out volunteers who are willing to faithfully serve in various capacities in line with their gifting and ability. This includes opportunities for those who prefer to serve quietly in the background. While stuffing envelopes or cleaning restrooms may seem disconnected from the concept of this chapter, serving the Lord in any tangible way is an integral part of becoming a blessing. Volunteering in the church means much more than fulfilling mundane tasks just to fill time. It is about serving God and making ourselves available to help accomplish the vision of the local body.

Similar to local churches, many cities also have ministries that are in need of volunteers. You can serve in places like homeless shelters, soup kitchens and nursing homes. This provides an opportunity to bless people who are going through a challenging time in their lives and to share the love of Christ with them. Getting involved in volunteer service will provide you with a sense of purpose, fill your time with meaningful activities and put your focus onto something outside of yourself.

Start a Small Group

Many churches offer small groups as an extension of their ministries. Developing a smaller community creates a context that is conducive to deeper and more meaningful relationships than can be developed on a typical Sunday morning. Our family has led several of these groups over the years, and each of them has been a season of growth and an opportunity to pour into the lives of others. Taking the time to pray, study Scripture and have open discussion creates an environment that fosters maturity and community. The danger in just attending service on Sunday morning is that you can fade into the background and avoid any true sense of fellowship or accountability. Having a small group of people that you are in community with provides a sense of protection that is important to walking in freedom. Consider starting a small group where you can get to know others on a deeper level and pray for and encourage them in their faith journey.

Start a Men's Accountability Group

Chapter 14 highlighted the need to have ongoing accountability relationships with other men—something that I have found does not typically occur in the church. It requires a man who will champion the cause and intentionally invite other men to join. Whether that is a weekly, biweekly or monthly meeting is determined by the willingness and ability of the men involved. You can meet anywhere, such as in a home, coffee shop or restaurant. The details are flexible, but the core purpose for the group is to give men the opportunity to share what is truly going on in their lives. Leading an accountability group is a great way to share the principles the Lord has taught you with other men.

Organize a Men's Purity Event

One great way to provide an opportunity for men to deal with pornography in their lives is to organize an event specifically aimed at purity. There are two primary ways to accomplish this. First, you can schedule a one-session event, such as a men's breakfast or special service. You can also host a weekend event, with several sessions dealing with topics relating to men. I have personally spoken at many of these types of events designed to tackle the "elephant in the room." It gives men a chance to be confronted but also offers them hope and resources to help them get out of sexual sin. I have seen how powerful these events can be as a catalyst for men to reach out for help.

A second option is to launch a several-week study on the topic of purity. This is a group that meets for a designated time with the intent of tackling the issues that men face with sexual sin. Pure Life Ministries offers a video series by Steve Gallagher called, *20 Truths that Helped Me in My Battle with Porn*.[3] They also published a 40-day workbook with the same title that works in conjunction with the video series. Each day provides the testimony of a man who has come into freedom as well as a Bible study and teaching. A similar study could be done with *Delete*. Appendix E has an explanation of how to accomplish a several-week study with this resource.

Within these study groups, men have a chance to hear the Word of

God and be encouraged to walk in freedom. A study group provides a great opportunity to ask questions and have discussions regarding the topic.

The Rescue Plan

After working through the process outlined in this book, some men will have a desire to take part in an important work that I refer to as *The Rescue Plan*. Essentially, this involves coming alongside a man who is struggling with porn in an effort to help lead him into freedom. This is for men who have established a solid foundation of victory and are in a place to be able to help someone else through the process. *The Rescue Plan* begins by asking the Lord to send you a man you can help. Once that happens, you have an initial conversation with him to gauge his willingness. If he seems committed, then you would meet with him on a weekly basis to go through the material of *Delete*, as well as help him implement the principles we have discussed. This counseling-type relationship lasts for a pre-determined timeframe. As you are working with a man, you will help him establish a good accountability system to maintain his freedom once *The Rescue Plan* is finished. Then, you will pray for God to send another man to rescue.

The specific details of how to do *The Rescue Plan* are provided in Appendix F. You will find it to be a very messy but rewarding ministry. If you are just now fighting your way out of porn, you are not ready to undertake this commitment, but the day will come when you can!

God's desire for every man reading these words is to make his life an incredible blessing on this earth. That process has been hindered in the past by your addiction to pornography. As you begin to walk in true freedom, the possibilities to share the love of Christ and reflect His glory are endless. He wants to take your life and make it a blessing to others. Hopefully, some of these ideas will stir up your desire to get out of yourself and begin to serve the Lord and other people. As you do, what the enemy meant for evil in your life will be turned around for the good of others.

CHAPTER 16

Increase Volume:// become-a-blessing

PRAYER POINTS

- Pray that God will restore the lives of other men you know personally who have experienced destruction due to their sexual sin

- Pray for insight into how you can take your unique gifts and abilities and use them to create opportunities to share Jesus with others

- Pray that the Lord will make your life a blessing to others around you

DISCUSSION QUESTIONS

1. Why is it so important that a man who struggles with porn become others-focused? What will happen internally to the man who endeavors to become a blessing?

2.   The chapter states, "Imagine if every man in the church who has been set free from porn made it their personal mission to pray for other men in bondage and seek to share their testimony with them. The message that Jesus can set men free from sexual sin would spread throughout the Body of Christ exponentially." How can men practically apply this concept in their everyday lives?

3.   What is it about the process of repentance that positively impacts lives beyond the person experiencing it? How have you seen this play out in other situations?

4.   How can a man actively use his testimony of freedom to be a source of encouragement to other men who are still in bondage?

5.   What are some other ways that a man can get involved in serving not listed in this chapter?

PERSONAL APPLICATION QUESTIONS

1.   At this stage in your personal journey, what are the most applicable concepts in this chapter that you can put into practice right away?

2.   How do you hope to see the Lord use your own struggles to encourage others in the future? What needs to happen in your life to make that a possibility?

3.   Is it difficult for you to imagine the Lord making your life a rich source of blessing in the lives of other people right now? Why or why not?

Conclusion

End:// its-just-the-beginning

AS WE BRING *DELETE* TO A CLOSE, I trust that you have been given the inspiration to make the necessary changes to rid your life of porn once and for all. I have endeavored to be as transparent and candid as possible. I set out to write the kind of book that might have given me the breakthrough that I needed had I read it when I was in sin. While I cannot go back and change my past, I can certainly do everything in my ability to try to keep others from going the same route. That is the heart behind this book.

The question that every reader must ask himself now is: "What am I going to do with what I have received?" Simply setting this material down and walking away unchanged is unacceptable if there is still sexual sin in your life. A man can agree with the contents of a book, but his agreement is meaningless unless he takes specific action in response to it. James talks about the person who hears the Word of the Lord but does not put it into practice.[1] If the Lord is speaking to you through these pages, I want to strongly encourage you: "Don't be a hearer only; be an obey-er!" With that thought in mind, I want to share a story that I hope will encourage you to do everything it takes to get free, stay free and help other men find freedom.

There was a young man in our youth ministry many years ago after I graduated from Pure Life Ministries. We were having special services at our church one night, and he asked to meet with me in private. He shared that he had secretly gotten hooked on porn at a younger age, and he felt such conviction that night that he knew he needed to tell someone. Knowing my testimony and trusting me as his youth pastor, he decided to confide in me. He seemed desperate, and I was grateful that he had the courage to confess.

I spent time counseling him, helping him confess to his parents. He eventually experienced repentance and found true freedom. Over the last few years, it has been an incredible experience to watch him mature into a man of God. He is now married, serving as a youth pastor and has two kids of his own. He is actively leading other young men into the same freedom that he experienced. His family is taking steps to become missionaries. Only God knows the amazing things that He will accomplish through this man's life. His story has been a vivid illustration of what healthy repentance looks like. By confessing at a young age, he was able to avoid a great deal of pain as he entered into his marriage and ministry in purity.

This story represents the way that repentance is supposed to unfold. This young man, hopelessly bound by porn, went through the process described in this book. He brought his sin into the light, closed the door to temptation, sought the Lord with a sincere heart and submitted himself to godly counsel. Over the years, he has lived within designated boundaries, maintained accountability around him and is now helping to rescue others out of sin. This is what God makes possible through the powerful process of repentance!

I wish I could report that his experience is what I have seen happen in the life of every porn-addicted man with whom I have come into contact. Unfortunately, I could tell many stories of men who have refused to implement the principles in this book and remained in the grip of sin. There have been men who have confessed to me secretly and yet refused to be open with others in their lives. They have paid a dear price for their refusal to truly bring their sin into the light. There are others who would not do the necessary work of fully closing the doors to temptation who are still bound today. I have tried to counsel men who would not take their bondage seriously, deciding instead to go their own way, refusing to apply the Scriptures to their lives. Some of these men who once claimed to be Christians are no longer in the church but have given themselves completely over to their sin. Even as I am writing these words, my heart breaks for them, and I pray the Lord will get a hold of their hearts and set them free. However, their story does not have to be *your* story.

You will choose which type of man you will be. Your story can tell about a man who was courageous enough to do everything it took to get free from porn, or it can be one of continuous defeat. The tragedy about putting off the decision to change is that you never know if another chance will be given. If everything that we have talked about in this book is true, then your very eternity could be at stake. My advice to every man reading these words is the same that Jesus' mother spoke at the wedding in Cana: "Whatever He says to you, do it."[2]

Know that I have prayed for you before you began reading the first words of this book. I do not believe that you are reading this by chance, accident or coincidence. The Holy Spirit has drawn you to this moment. Now, do what He says to do, and watch Him do in your life what only He can do! If you decide you need to pursue a residential or at-home counseling ministry, please use the contact information for Pure Life Ministries in the back of the book. They specialize in helping men and women overcome sexual sin and have been doing so effectively for nearly forty years.

May the Lord bless you richly as you endeavor to walk through the process of repentance and delete porn from your life once and for all to the glory of God!

Plus:// appendices

APPENDIX A: RESOURCES FOR PURITY

Based on the principles of closing the door to temptation in Chapter 10 and building a wall of protection in Chapter 13, I want to provide specific resources to help you accomplish those goals. As a disclaimer, I want to mention that the following content was assembled with information that was current at the time of this writing. With technology rapidly changing, some of this material may become outdated after printing. Please do your research before selecting any of these options to ensure it is best for you and your situation. Many of these companies offer both hardware and software options, and each product has its own features and limitations. So, a visit to each website is important to examine the resources available. Also, I have no personal or professional connection to any of the companies listed other than ArkCybr, so listing them here is not necessarily an endorsement of their product or service.

Professional and Customized Assistance:

If you have any questions about how to properly eliminate access to porn, filter websites, or setup parental controls on any of your devices, I highly recommend you reach out to ArkCybr. Founded by a graduate of Pure Life Ministries, this company offers consultations with people who need help with their devices as well as an online course to help walk you through that process. For a fee, you can reach out to ArkCybr and they can help navigate the complexities of blocking porn from the internet coming into your home, smart TVs, game systems and other devices that can be difficult to filter. In fact, they can help filter your internet before it comes into your home. I have made frequent requests to ArkCybr over the years and their help has been invaluable to my personal protection. Especially for those who are technologically deficient, or even those who have too much IT knowledge, ArkCybr can be a great resource for a customized approach to your technological needs. Website: **arkcybr.com**

Software Options:

Accountability and Filtering:

- CovenantEyes (covenanteyes.com)

- Qustodio (qustodio.com)

- Accountable2You (accountable2you.com)

- Net Nanny (netnanny.com)

Hardware Options:

Routers:

- Gryphon AX (gryphonconnect.com)

- Vilo Router (store.viloliving.com)

Porn Free Phones:

- MM Guardian Phone (mmguardian.com/kids-phone)

- Bark Home- (bark.us)

- Gabb (gabb.com)

- Techless Wisephone (wisephone.com)

APPENDIX B: REX ANDREWS' MERCY PRAYER

As discussed in Chapter 11, praying for others is an effective way to overcome lust and other heart issues. The following is a prayer pattern that will help you develop this discipline in your life. Some of the wording might seem awkward, such as the usage of "Mercy them" and "Life them." These are expressed this way intentionally to stay true to the way the biblical languages express these actions as verbs.

- Lord, I thank you for (name of person). I thank You for saving them. Thank You for what You have done and are doing in their life.

- Make (name of person) to know Jesus. Help them to increase in the knowledge of God. Destroy speculations and every lofty thing raised up against the knowledge of God and help them to bring every thought captive to the obedience of Christ.

- Make (name of person) poor in spirit. Bring them down, Lord, but do it gently. Help them to see their neediness. Help (name of person) to see themself in light of You. Put (name of person) in their rightful place, Lord.

- Fill (name of person) with Your Holy Spirit. Immerse them in Your Spirit, Lord. Come to them in power and might. Baptize them in fire, Lord.

- Life (name of person). Life them according to Thy lovingkindness. Pour out Your life-giving mercies into their soul.

- Bless (name of person). Lord, bless them in everything they touch. Bless them spiritually, physically and financially. Bless their loved ones. Do for them, Lord, instead of me.

- Mercy (name of person). Flood them with need-filling mercies. Pour them out in super abundance. Find and meet every need in their life as you see it, Lord.[1]

APPENDIX C: BIBLICAL COUNSELING
ORGANIZATIONS

The following is a list of recommended counseling organizations with their websites. Do some research before selecting an organization to ensure that they offer the type of counseling that best fits your situation:

- The Association of Certified Biblical Counselors (ACBC) (biblicalcounseling.com)

- International Association of Biblical Counselors (IABC) (iabc.net)

- Fellowship of Biblical Counselors (FBC) (fbcounselors.com)

PURE LIFE MINISTRIES

Pure Life offers a residential program for men, phone counseling for struggling men and women as well as hurting wives, and a variety of written and digital resources. I highly encourage you to contact them for more information:

888-PURELIFE

Pure Life Ministries
14 School St.
Dry Ridge, KY 41035

purelifeministries.org

APPENDIX D: MEN'S ACCOUNTABILITY QUESTIONS

Below is a list of questions that are great conversation starters for accountability relationships. The first set is directed specifically toward sexual purity. The second set comes from Patrick Morley's book "Man in the Mirror." You can find these questions printed on small cards to keep in your wallet at their website (maninthemirror.org). Morley's questions include other areas of a man's life beyond sexuality. As your accountability relationship grows, I recommend that each man write down and share a list of personal questions that target his unique struggles that are not included in this list. This will ensure he is being asked the most important questions for his situation.

Accountability Questions Specific to Sexual Sin:

- Have you looked at anything sexual since we last met?

- Where are you fighting temptation the most?

- How are you handling your imagination in regard to lustful thoughts?

- How are you doing with masturbation?

- Do you have any relationships that are becoming too close or are a source of temptation?

Men's Accountability Questions
Taken from Patrick Morley's Book "Man in the Mirror"

Opening questions

- How has God blessed you this week? (What went right?)

- What problem has consumed your thoughts this week? (What went wrong?)

Spiritual Questions

- Have you read God's Word daily? (How long? Why not? Will you next week?)

- Describe your prayers? (for yourself, others, praise confession, gratitude)

- How is your relationship with Christ changing?

- How have you been tempted this week? How did you respond?

- Do you have any unconfessed sin in your life?

- Are you walking by the Holy Spirit?

- Did you worship in church this week? (Was your faith in Christ strengthened? Was God glorified and honored?)

- Have you shared your faith? In what ways? How can you improve?

Home Life

- How is it going with your wife? (attitudes, time, irritations, disappointments, progress, her relationship with Christ)

- How is it going with the children? (quantity and quality time, values and beliefs, education, spiritual welfare)

- How are your finances doing? (debt, sharing, saving, stewardship)

- How have you invested your time around the house?

Work Life

- How are things going on the job? (career progress, relationships, temptations, workload, stress, problems, working too much)

Critical concerns

- Do you feel in the center of God's will? Do you sense His peace?

- What are you wrestling with in your thought life?

- What have you done for someone else this week? (encouragement, service, etc.)

- Are your priorities in the right order?

- Is your moral and ethical behavior what it should be?

- How are you doing in your personal high-risk area?

- Is the "visible" you and the "real" you consistent?

Visit maninthemirror.org for more resources for men

APPENDIX E: HOW TO USE *DELETE* AS A GROUP STUDY

For those who desire to use *Delete* in a group setting, below are two potential schedules as well as some basic guidelines to set a foundation for the study. Each can be tweaked depending on the length of the study and the specific dynamics of your group.

Plan for an 8-Week Study

- **Week 1:** Introduction and Chapters 1 and 2
- **Week 2:** Chapters 3 and 4
- **Week 3:** Chapters 5 and 6
- **Week 4:** Chapters 7 and 8
- **Week 5:** Chapters 9 and 10
- **Week 6:** Chapters 11 and 12
- **Week 7:** Chapters 13 and 14
- **Week 8:** Chapters 15 and 16 and Conclusion

Plan for a 12-Week Study

- **Week 1:** Introduction and Chapter 1
- **Week 2:** Chapters 2 and 3
- **Week 3:** Chapter 4
- **Week 4:** Chapter 5
- **Week 5:** Chapters 6 and 7
- **Week 6:** Chapter 8
- **Week 7:** Chapter 9
- **Week 8:** Chapter 10
- **Week 9:** Chapters 11 and 12
- **Week 10:** Chapter 13
- **Week 11:** Chapters 14 and 15
- **Week 12:** Chapter 16 and Conclusion

In each meeting, there are three main elements that should be included:

1. Prayer

Spending time in prayer together as a group is a powerful way to invite the Holy Spirit into each man's situation. Every man will be coming to your group in a different place spiritually. As a facilitator, your primary responsibility is to give God an opportunity to minister to the men right where they are. Praying over each meeting ahead of time, during the meeting and after it takes place will help maximize the effectiveness of the group throughout the weeks of the study. You can also use the prayer points in each chapter as a guide for specific prayer targets during the meeting.

2. Discussion About the Book

Delete was written with discussion questions to be used in a group setting. As you are reading through the content ahead of the meeting, highlight sections that stand out to you and any discussion points you think will be pertinent to the men. Depending on the length of each meeting, you can tailor the discussion segment to match your setting. You want to provide a few boundaries to help direct the discussion. Examples would be asking men to allow others to share and to not dominate the discussion time, keeping their answers on topic as well as to avoid sharing unnecessary details that can cause another brother to stumble.

3. Personal Reflection

Providing a chance for personal reflection can be accomplished in several ways. Each chapter provides a few personal application questions to help bring the content closer to home. For large groups, it might be helpful to break the men up into smaller groups to create a less intimidating atmosphere to share about their personal journey. It should be emphasized that what is shared is confidential (within legal boundaries) and men should not use this time to just dump their sin on the group. These discussion groups should be given specific questions to answer each week in order to keep them on track. In a smaller group study, it may not be necessary to break the group down into smaller sections, and these questions can be provided to the entire group.

Maintaining Follow-Up

There will be men who come to your group study, and God will use it to help them expose their sin and reach out for help. You should have a system in place in advance to help him walk through this process. This could involve you personally making yourself available and meeting with him separate from the group. Or it could be that you have other godly men prepared to walk him through the process of repentance. Be ready ahead of time so that if a man reaches out for help, there is a system in place to address their issues immediately, because once a man opens that door, it is important to "strike while the iron is hot" before he changes his mind. This preparation might include pointing a man to specific resources for counsel, such as a pastor, biblical counselor or Pure Life Ministries if his situation is more challenging than you or your leadership team can handle.

APPENDIX F: THE RESCUE PLAN

The Rescue Plan is reserved for men who find themselves in a place of freedom and maturity after going through the principles of *Delete*. Not every man is ready or gifted to walk through this process with other men. Mentoring others requires stability and spiritual maturity as well as the desire and ability to help. This process should be done under the direction of a spiritual leader in your life, who can discern where you are personally in your journey and can help direct you as you seek to minister to other men. For those who are prepared to take on this work, I want to provide a simple six-step process that you can use to initiate and facilitate *The Rescue Plan*.

Step 1: Pray for One Man to Rescue

The process of rescuing other men out of pornography must be bathed in prayer. The Holy Spirit can bring the right man or men along your path. You are not merely looking for a man who professes Christ and is hooked on porn. Instead, you want to find one who is also prepared to do the hard work of change. There is a big difference between the two, and praying for discernment is key. Make this an intentional point of prayer. Ask God to put a man in your life who needs to find freedom from porn. Pray that you will have opportunities to share your story with other men. Do not overthink the process. After all, the Lord is much more concerned with a man's availability than his ability to have all the answers. Make yourself available and then look for the answer to your prayer through the men you come into contact with.

Step 2: Throw Out a Lifeline

Not every man is ready to confess his sin without being prompted. I have found that someone else often needs to initiate an opportunity for men to confess. A practical way to do this is to tell a man you know something like, "Hey, I've been praying that the Lord would connect me with men who want to learn how to walk in greater purity in their lives. I thought of you and wanted to see if that is something you'd be interested in."

There are many creative ways to give opportunities for men to come into the light. For example, I recently told the guys at our accountability breakfast, "If you are struggling with porn and you want to get free, I'm throwing out a lifeline to you guys to reach out to me directly and let's take care of this now." Find ways to communicate that you are available and want to join forces with men to help them get free. A simple conversation can open a man's heart in a powerful way. You will be amazed at the doors that will open if you simply make yourself available.

Step 3: Have an Initial Conversation

As you work through the first two steps, this one will come with time. I have found that setting up a meeting to assess a man's situation and determine the best course of action is essential. This should happen before you make any kind of ongoing commitment. There are a variety of factors that play into that initial conversation. During the meeting, you are trying to gauge how deep into porn the man is and whether his situation extends beyond your ability to help him. Questions like the following are instrumental in diagnosing the situation:

- How often are you looking at pornography?

- Are you married? If so, does your wife know anything?

- Does anyone else know about this other than you and me?

- Does any of your pornography usage crossed over into illegal activity?

- Have you acted out with other people, either physically or through a digital device?

While there is always a risk that a man will lie about some of the information, it is still helpful to ask the questions. Based on his answers, you can determine whether you need to refer him to a program like Pure Life Ministries, directly to a biblical counselor, or try to walk through the process with him yourself. At the end of the meeting, you will have to make the decision prayerfully about whether you want to try to take him under your wing or if you feel that a referral will be a better fit.

Step 4: Initiate The Rescue Plan

If you feel like the Lord is leading you to work with a man after the initial conversation, you should set up a weekly appointment for about an hour and have him go through the contents of *Delete*. Each week, his assignment is to read through a chapter and answer the discussion and personal application questions on paper. This will give him something tangible to do between meetings and provide material for discussion. Initially, the top priority is getting him to expose his sin to his wife (if married) and making sure all his devices are locked down. Then, how seriously he engages with the material will determine how successful the process is.

Along with the bookwork, he should be expected to spend time with God in prayer and Scripture interaction each day. This is something you should ask him about in each meeting to gauge his spiritual growth. If he is not willing to spend time with the Lord on a consistent basis, that reveals that he is not serious, and you should discontinue the plan until he is ready to do what he needs to do spiritually. If he is sincerely trying, yet struggling in consistency, that is a different situation, and you can talk through the reasons for it and offer support to help him.

You must be prepared to walk through messy terrain, but if the man is serious, he will get free. If he is showing signs that he is not ready such as refusing to be transparent, an unwillingness to lock down his devices, missing appointments or not reading the book, you should terminate the accountability relationship. I have had to have that difficult conversation with men in the past. Essentially, a man like that needs to understand that you are not willing to waste your time as well as his when he will not follow your counsel. Sometimes men confess under the emotional burden they are feeling but are not actually ready to do what it takes when the time comes. Pray for these men that the Lord will change their hearts and that they will truly repent. But realize that in some situations, you will want to see a man get free more than he desires that freedom. In such cases, pray and move on to a man who is ready.

Going through *The Rescue Plan* with a man is meant to fulfill the need for biblical counseling in Chapter 12. With the material provided in the book, the hope is that he will not need to find a more formal counseling relationship. However, if a man's situation becomes more than you can handle, refer him to Pure Life Ministries. Ideally, he should go to the residential program if possible. But there is also an at-home phone program available that can be effective for men who cannot go to the residential program.

One of the most difficult parts of this work is walking through the destruction that is caused to the wives of married men. While I have often had initial conversations with a man and his wife, I am only able to provide ongoing support to the husband. Sometimes, my wife will take the man's spouse under her care, but often, I will encourage the wife to get her own counsel. There are a myriad of emotions and difficult decisions to make, and a wife needs to have someone who can come alongside her in the process. Finding a biblical counselor for her can be extremely helpful. Pure Life Ministries also has a phone program designed specifically for hurting wives that can be very beneficial if she is willing to go through it.

Step 5: Setup an Ongoing Accountability System

Once a man that you are working with completes the material after roughly three to four months, and there is evidence that he is applying the principles to his life, he needs to have an ongoing accountability relationship established. If you have the time and ability to continue meeting with the man after *The Rescue Plan* is completed, by all means, continue to keep him accountable. Chapter 14 should have already convinced him of his need for this kind of relationship. Due to limited time and ministry responsibilities, I am not able to be an ongoing support to many of the men I have worked with through this process. However, it is essential that every man has someone that is asking the tough questions and checking in on him periodically. Do your best to make sure this is in place before your meetings are over. It can be helpful to sit down together including the new accountability partner to "pass the torch" and share about the man's progress.

While not every man you choose to meet with will find freedom right away, some of them will. Here is an example of how the process looks when successful. Not long ago, I had a conversation about my ministry with a man who I have known for many years. He called me shortly after that conversation and said that he was extremely convicted when I shared about how I have seen men get free from porn because of his own battle. Although he was sixty-years old and had not battled with pornography in the past, a year prior to our conversation, he had stumbled into porn on the internet and had gotten himself hooked. The Lord knew that he needed to hear what I had to share with him.

We began to get together for *The Rescue Plan*. I helped him lock down his devices and began to receive accountability reports from his internet usage. We studied *At the Altar of Sexual Idolatry* and went through all the steps in this book, which led to some great discussions. We prayed together on a regular basis, and I helped him walk through his questions and concerns along the way. Eventually, we stopped meeting as often and I have stayed in touch with him to provide ongoing accountability. I am so grateful to the Lord that he has been able to walk in freedom for over two years. He will be able to continue for the rest of his life if he chooses to keep implementing the principles we have outlined and can eventually take part in reaching other men if he chooses.

Step 6: Help Equip Other Men

If we continue to raise up godly men with a burden for those in the church who are hooked on porn, we can make a significant change to the epidemic. Once you have walked through this process with a couple of guys, you will get a feel for the intricacies of this work. Now, you can be used by the Lord to recruit other men to do the same. As you will have learned by that point in the process, it takes a certain level of maturity and gifting to do this work effectively. You should look for men who have deep compassion, are willing to lovingly confront and are walking in freedom themselves. Then, you can go through this process together so they can learn first-hand what it takes.

One thing I know about men is that we want our lives to count. We want to walk in purpose and make a difference in this world. What greater work can a man do than pluck souls out of the grips of Satan and help walk them in freedom so that they can be the men, husbands and fathers God has called them to be? It is a big task, so we need as many hands on deck as possible.

So, what about you? Are you in a place where you have experienced freedom from pornography? Are you willing to begin to pray and ask the Lord to send men your way who you can link arms with and help find freedom? Thank you in advance to those who will accept this challenge and step into the trenches to fight for the souls of other men.

NOTES

Chapter 1:

1. John Uri, 2020. "50 Years Ago: 'Houston, We've Had a Problem.'" *NASA.* Accessed online at https://www.nasa.gov/history/50-years-ago-houston-weve-had-a-problem.

2. "Epidemic." *EFSA,* 2025. Accessed online at https://www.efsa.europa.eu/en/glossary/epidemic.

3. Proven Men. "Pornography Survey Statistics." Accessed online at https://www.provenmen.org/pornography-survey-statistics-2014.

4. Hannah Harrison. "Porn and the Church." *AFA Journal.* Accessed online at https://afajournal.org/past-issues/2020/october/porn-and-the-church.

5. The Barna Group, 2024. *Beyond the Porn Phenomenon,* p. 6. PDF Download.

6. Proven Men. "Pornography Survey Statistics." Accessed online at https://www.provenmen.org/pornography-survey-statistics-2014.

7. The Barna Group, 2016. *The Porn Phenomenon.* Accessed online at https://www.barna.com/the-porn-phenomenon.

8. The Barna Group, 2024. *Beyond the Porn Phenomenon,* p. 14. PDF Download.

9. Joseph H. Thayer. *Thayer's Greek-English Lexicon of the New Testament.* (Grand Rapids, MI: 1977) p. 448, ref. no. 3687.

10. Hebrews 3:15 (emphasis mine)

11. Job 1:7

12. "What's the Average Age of a Child's First Exposure to Porn?" *Fight the New Drug.* Accessed online at https://fightthenewdrug.org/real-average-age-of-first-exposure.

13. "Your Conversation Blueprint" *Fight the New Drug.* Accessed online at https://fightthenewdrug.org/lets-talk-about-porn/blueprint/child-gen.

14. The Barna Group, 2016. *The Porn Phenomenon.* Accessed online at https://www.barna.com/the-porn-phenomenon.

Chapter 2:

1. 1 Peter 2:9

2. 2 Corinthians 5:17

Chapter 3:

1. Clive Staples Lewis. *Mere Christianity*. (Hammersmith, London: HarperCollins, 1952) p. 104.

2. The Barna Group, 2024. *Beyond the Porn Phenomenon*, p. 35. PDF Download.

3. ibid., p. 35.

4. "Pornography and your Christian Marriage." *Dr. Carol Ministries*. Accessed online at https://www.drcarolministries.com/pornography-and-your-christian-marriage.

5. "How Porn Can Negatively Impact Love and Intimacy." *Fight the New Drug*. Accessed online at https://fightthenewdrug.org/how-porn-negatively-impact-relationship.

Chapter 4:

1. Exodus 20:17, 14

2. The Barna Group, 2024. *Beyond the Porn Phenomenon*, p. 42-43. PDF Download.

3. Tré Goins-Phillips, 2024. "Majority of Christians Confess to Using Porn—And Many Are Comfortable With It, Study Finds." *Faithwire*. Accessed at https://www.faithwire.com/2024/10/22/majority-of-christians-confess-to-using-porn-and-many-are-comfortable-with-it-study-finds.

4. Bible Hub. "Porneia." *Helps Word Studies*, 2011. Ref. no. 4202. Accessed online at https://biblehub.com/greek/4202.htm.

5. 1 Corinthians 5:5

6. Romans 8:13

7. Joseph H. Thayer. *Thayer's Greek-English Lexicon of the New Testament*. (Grand Rapids, MI: 1977) p. 21, ref. no. 167.

8. Colossians 3:5 NIV

9. Bible Hub. "Pathos." *Helps Word Studies*, 2011. Ref. no. 3806. Accessed online at https://biblehub.com/greek/3806.htm.

10. 1 Corinthians 6:18 NIV

11. Joseph H. Thayer. *Thayer's Greek-English Lexicon of the New Testament*. (Grand Rapids, MI: 1977) p. 651, ref. no. 5343.

12. Genesis 39

13. Bible Hub. "Planaó." *Helps Word Studies*, 2011. Ref. no. 4105. Accessed online at https://biblehub.com/greek/4105.htm.

14. Colossians 3:6

15. Jeremiah 17:9 NIV

Chapter 5:

1. Bible Hub. "Phthora." *Helps Word Studies*, 2011. Ref. no. 5356. Accessed online at https://biblehub.com/greek/5356.htm.

2. "How Porn Can Harm Consumers' Sex Lives." *Fight the New Drug*. Accessed online at https://fightthenewdrug.org/how-porn-can-harm-consumers-sex-lives.

3. "How Porn Can Normalize Sexual Objectification." *Fight the New Drug*. Accessed online at https://fightthenewdrug.org/how-porn-can-normalize-sexual-objectification.

4. Joseph H. Thayer. *Thayer's Greek-English Lexicon of the New Testament*. (Grand Rapids, MI: 1977) p. 452, ref. no. 3715.

5. Rex Andrews. *What the Bible Teaches About Mercy*. (Zion, Illinois: Zion Faith Homes, 1985) p. unknown.

6. Matthew 15:19

7. 1 Corinthians 7:9

8. "Internet Pornography by the Numbers." *Webroot*. Accessed online at https://www.webroot.com/us/en/resources/tips-articles/internet-pornography-by-the-numbers.

9. "9 Surprising Facts about Human Trafficking in the U.S." *Fight the New Drug*. Accessed online at https://fightthenewdrug.org/surprising-facts-about-human-trafficking-in-the-u-s.

10. Keith Rose, 2023. "Porn and Sex Trafficking: Is There a Connection?'" *Covenant Eyes*. Accessed online at https://www.covenanteyes.com/blog/porn-and-sex-trafficking-10-facts-from-the-experts.

11. Taylor Tennis, 2021. "Porn and Human Trafficking: The Facts You Need to Know." *The Exodus Road*. Accessed online at https://theexodusroad.com/porn-and-human-trafficking-the-facts-you-need-to-know.

12. ibid.

13. Keith Rose, 2023. "Porn and Sex Trafficking: Is There a Connection?'" *Covenant Eyes*. Accessed online at https://www.covenanteyes.com/blog/porn-and-sex-trafficking-10-facts-from-the-experts.

14. "How Common is Sexual Violence in Porn?" *Fight the New Drug*. Accessed online at https://fightthenewdrug.org/how-common-is-sexual-violence-in-porn.

Chapter 6:

1. 2 Samuel 12:24-25

2. 1 Kings 3:3

3. 1 Kings 3:11-13

4. 1 Kings 4:25

5. 1 Kings 3:1

6. 1 Kings 10:28

7. 1 Kings 3:12

8. 1 Kings 3:26

9. 1 Kings 3:28

10. 1 Kings 4:34

11. 1 Kings 10:7

12. James 1:22

13. Thomas à Kempis. *The Imitation of Christ*. (Grand Rapids, MI: Christian Classics Ethereal Library, 1400) p. 11.

14. 1 Kings 11:1-3

15. Bible Hub. "Dabaq." *Brown-Driver-Briggs Hebrew and English Lexicon*, 2006. Accessed online at https://biblehub.com/hebrew/1692.htm.

16. 1 Kings 11:43

Chapter 7:

1. 1 Samuel 17:34-36

2. 1 Samuel 17

3. Examples include: 1 Samuel 18:1; 18:17, 21; 19:1; 19:10-11; 26:2

4. 1 Samuel 18:5

5. 2 Samuel 12:5

6. 2 Samuel 12:5-6

7. 2 Samuel 12:13

8. Examples include: Jeremiah 37:15–16; 1 Kings 19:1–14; Daniel 6; 1 Kings 19:10; Matthew 23:35

9. See Matthew 1:1; Matthew 12:23; Matthew 21:9; Luke 18:38

Chapter 8:

1. Bible Hub. "Checed." *Topical Encyclopedia*. Accessed online at https://biblehub.com/hebrew/2617.htm.

2. Bible Hub. "Racham." *Strong's Lexicon*. Accessed online at https://biblehub.com/hebrew/7355.htm.

3. ibid.

4. Bible Hub. "Pesha." *Strong's Lexicon*. Accessed online at https://biblehub.com/hebrew/6588.htm.

5. Bible Hub. "Avon." *Strong's Lexicon*. Accessed online at https://biblehub.com/hebrew/5771.htm.

6. Bible Hub. "Chatta'ah." *Strong's Lexicon*. Accessed online at https://biblehub.com/hebrew/2403.htm.

7. Bible Hub. "Machah." *Strong's Lexicon*. Accessed online at https://biblehub.com/hebrew/4229.htm.

8. C. H. Spurgeon. "Psalm 51." *Blue Letter Bible*. Accessed online at https://www.blueletterbible.org/Comm/spurgeon_charles/tod/ps051.cfm.

9. John Piper, 2008. "A Broken and Contrite Heart God Will Not Despise." *Desiring God*. Accessed online at https://www.desiringgod.org/messages/a-broken-and-contrite-heart-god-will-not-despise.

10. Bible Hub. "Kun." *Brown-Driver-Briggs Hebrew and English Lexicon*, 2006. Accessed online at https://biblehub.com/hebrew/3559.htm.

11. 1 Samuel 16:14

12. C. H. Spurgeon. "Psalm 51." *Grace Gems*. Accessed online at https://gracegems.org/Spurgeon/051.htm.

13. 2 Corinthians 7:10

14. ibid.

15. Charles Finney. *How to Experience Revival*. (New Kensington, PA: Whitaker House, 1984) p. 101-102.

Chapter 9:

1. Steve Gallagher. *At the Altar of Sexual Idolatry*. (Dry Ridge, KY: Pure Life Ministries, 2007) p. 68.

2. Romans 1:24

3. Bernard of Clairvaux. As cited online, quote accessed at: https://www.azquotes.com/quote/767449.

4. 2 Corinthians 6:2

5. Hebrews 3:15

Chapter 10:

1. The Barna Group, 2016. *The Porn Phenomenon*. Accessed online at https://www.barna.com/the-porn-phenomenon.

2. "Virtual Reality and Immersive Adult Experiences." 2023. *Medium*. Accessed online at https://medium.com/@topbosstalk/virtual-reality-and-immersive-adult-experiences-615c37443375.

3. Kate Knibbs, 2024. "OpenAI Is 'Exploring' How to Responsibly Generate AI Porn." *Wired*. Accessed online at https://www.wired.com/story/openai-is-exploring-how-to-responsibly-generate-ai-porn.

4. "Introducing a Special Preview of the MetaMansion, Playboy's Iconic Landmark in the Metaverse." 2024. *Medium*. Accessed online at https://sandboxgame.medium.com/introducing-a-special-preview-of-the-metamansion-playboys-iconic-landmark-in-the-metaverse-dd26f012645a.

5. Ben Weiss, 2024. "Can AI Porn be Ethical?" *The Guardian*. Accessed online at https://www.theguardian.com/technology/2024/feb/18/ethics-ai-porn.

Chapter 11:

1. 2 Corinthians 13:5

2. Bible Hub. "Revelation 2:5." *Barnes' Notes on the Bible*. Accessed online at https://biblehub.com/commentaries/revelation/2-5.htm.

3. Matthew 6:1-18

4. John 14:15

5. Bible Hub. "Phroureó." *Helps Word Studies*, 2011. Ref. no. 5432. Accessed online at https://biblehub.com/greek/5432.htm.

6. Ibid., *Strong's Lexicon*.

7. Bible Hub. "Matthew 26:41." *Matthew Poole's Commentary*. Accessed online at https://biblehub.com/commentaries/matthew/26-41.htm.

8. William Law. *A Serious Call to a Devout and Holy Life*. (Philadelphia, PA: The Westminster Press, 1955) p. 76.

9. Matthew 17:21

10. 2 Samuel 12:16

11. Matthew 15:8

12. Steve Gallagher. *At the Altar of Sexual Idolatry*. (Dry Ridge, KY: Pure Life Ministries, 2007) p. 24.

13. Rex Andrews. *What the Bible Teaches About Mercy*. (Zion, Illinois: Zion Faith Homes, 1985) p. 205.

14. Rex Andrews. *What the Bible Teaches About Mercy*. (Zion, Illinois: Zion Faith Homes, 1985) p. 169.

Chapter 12:

1. 2 Timothy 3:16 NIV

2. 2 Peter 1:21

3. 1 Corinthians 15:56-57

4. Romans 7:24-25

5. Isaiah 55:9

6. Martin Luther. As cited online, quote accessed at: https://gracequotes.org/author-quote/martin-luther.

7. C. H. Spurgeon. As cited online, quote accessed at: https://gracequotes.org/author-quote/c-h-spurgeon.

8. Psalm 119:9

9. See Proverbs 5, 6, 7

10. Matthew 5:2

11. See Ephesians 5:3; 1 Corinthians 6:18; Romans 1:26-32

12. John 8:36

Chapter 13:

1. Luke 9:23

2. Ephesians 4:22-24; Colossians 3:9-10

3. "Walls of Jerusalem." *Wikipedia*. Accessed online at https://en.wikipedia.org/wiki/Walls_of_Jerusalem.

4. Jon Simpson, 2017. "Finding Brand Success In The Digital World." *Forbes*. Accessed online at https://www.forbes.com/sites/forbesagencycouncil/2017/08/25/finding-brand-success-in-the-digital-world.

5. 1 Thessalonians 4:3

Chapter 14:

1. Acts 4:36

2. Proverbs 27:17

3. Patrick Morley. *The Man in the Mirror.* (Grand Rapids, MI: Zondervan, 2014) p. 364.

4. Galatians 5:16

5. French Arrington. *The Act of the Apostles.* (Cleveland, TN: Pathway Press, 1998) p. 33.

6. Dietrich Bonhoeffer. As cited online, quote accessed at: https://gracequotes.org/author-quote/dietrich-bonhoeffer.

Chapter 15:

1. John 8

2. Luke 7

3. 2 Corinthians 10:5

4. Matthew 5:28

5. Sy Rogers. Spoken at a conference. Date and location unknown.

Chapter 16:

1. Genesis 50:20 NIV

2. Galatians 6:8 NIV

3. See https://www.purelifeministries.org/20-truths-series

Conclusion:

1. James 1:22

2. John 2:5

Appendices:

1. Rex Andrews. "The Mercy Prayer." Pure Life Ministries. Accessed online at https://www.purelifeministries.org/blog/podcast-victory-95-percent-of-mercy-is-prayer.

ABOUT THE AUTHOR

Dustin Renz is the Founder and President of Make Way Ministries and serves on the speaking team for Pure Life Ministries. He holds a Bachelor of Science in Church Ministries from Southeastern University in Lakeland, Florida. He is the author of *Pile of Masks: Exposing Christian Hypocrisy*, *The Crucified Lifestyle: Nine Practical Principles for the Cross-Centered Life* and the evangelistic novel, *Something Better*. He and his wife, Brittany, have three wonderful daughters and they currently reside in Kettering, Ohio.

Awakening the Church
to Evangelize the World

Make Way Ministries was established with the purpose of empowering the Body of Christ to awaken in revival, mature through discipleship and arise to evangelism as we make way for our soon-coming King, Jesus Christ. We accomplish this through our speaking, publishing and online ministries.

For more information about booking an event or to find resources, please visit us at www.makewayministries.com or email us at:
contact@makewayministries.com

MAKE WAY MINISTRIES

PILE *of* MASKS

LEARN HOW TO LIVE WITH
AN UNDIVIDED HEART!

Have you ever wondered why hypocrisy is so prevalent in the church? Many people have rejected the Christian faith due to the fact that they see nothing different in the lives of those who profess Christ and the rest of the world. The church is filled with the same issues that they face such as high divorce rates, drug and alcohol abuse, relational conflict, sexual immorality, fear of the future and an obsession with the things of this world. Is there any hope for a church culture that has grown lukewarm in its love for Jesus?

In Pile of Masks, Dustin Renz candidly explores this issue in the Christian community from an insider's vantage point. Having been set free from a hypocritical lifestyle himself, he explains how the Lord broke the chains of hypocrisy in his heart, restored his marriage and ministry and brought him into an authentic life in Christ.

This book takes readers on a journey through history to discover how the enemy has been using hypocrisy to pull people away from God since the beginning of time. It presents powerful principles to help all believers rise above a backslidden church culture. All who hunger for more than status quo Christianity need to read this book!

WWW.MAKEWAYMINISTRIES.COM

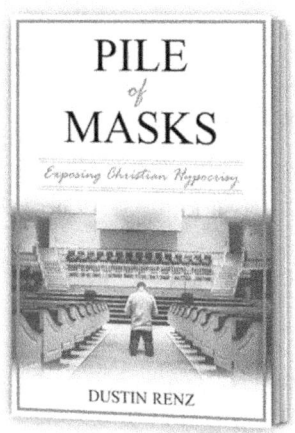

NOW ALSO AVAILABLE AS A VIDEO SERIES!

- 13 sessions from the book that is helping Christians find freedom from hypocrisy

- Over 4.5 hours of teaching

- Recorded in the Pure Life Ministries Chapel

WWW.MAKEWAYMINISTRIES.COM OR
WWW.YOUTUBE.COM/MAKEWAYMINISTRIES

THE **CRUCIFIED** LIFESTYLE

9 Practical Principles for the
Cross-Centered Life

Crucifixion.

An ancient form of capital punishment that is no longer practiced. Yet Jesus expected His followers to take up a cross. His call to discipleship was given many centuries ago. Times have changed…culture has changed…the world looks very different than when the Messiah's feet connected with the dust of the earth. But has the calling of a disciple changed with time and culture? Why is there such a seeming disparity between the experience of His original twelve disciples and the typical professing believer in today's church?

In *The Crucified Lifestyle*, Dustin Renz explores Jesus' call to discipleship in Luke 9:23 in search of answers to these questions. This book breathes fresh life into ancient biblical truths for the disciple in a twenty-first century context. Its pages contain nine relevant life-giving principles from the Scriptures that are essential for anyone who desires to follow Jesus.

If you long to find greater depth in your relationship with God and more freedom in your Christian walk, *The Crucified Lifestyle* provides a pathway to get you there. But beware, the truths contained within have the power to convict, challenge and transform your life!

"This is a must read book for all believers and is one that will be on my repeat list to continue to dig and reveal the gaps my own walk and trust in Jesus. You may be challenged reading this book… but great is His faithfulness in pulling us closer and pruning our hearts and life to be more like Him."
-**Joshua Plaisance (Amazon Review)**

WWW.MAKEWAYMINISTRIES.COM

SOMETHING
BETTER

He's lost his way and his family. Can a leap of faith bring them back together?

Tom Schneider's inner demons have cost him dearly. Still emotionally scarred from his abusive childhood, he fears he may never be the supportive husband and parent his family needs. After his wife takes their daughter and leaves, he wallows in his pain until his estranged father reaches out with a final dying wish.

Coping with his trauma and hopelessness, he returns to his Southern hometown in search of redemption. As he takes the winding path to self-discovery, he finds solace in a local church. But it's a chance encounter that might just renew his faith in a brighter future.

Will Tom forgive the sins of his past and open his heart to happiness?

Something Better is an inspirational Christian fiction story about the transformational power of redemption. If you like flawed heroes, tests of faith, and heartwarming journeys of rebirth, then you'll love Dustin Renz's second-chance saga.

WHAT OTHERS ARE SAYING ABOUT *SOMETHING BETTER:*

*"Renz has beautifully imagined a redemption story with believable
characters. Strongly recommended!"*

-(Goodreads Review)

*"The biblical message is strong as the main character discovers how real
Jesus really is. A very hopeful book. I highly recommend it!"*

-Christy (Amazon Review)

"What an incredible story of the path and power of redemption."

-Cinthia (Amazon Review)

*"So many books are forgettable, but this one will stay with me a while.
Tom's experience is so close to what I went through coming to Christ,
and the broken and redeemed marriage is so familiar. Renz made his
characters resonate with reality. Not many stories bring tears, but this
one did."*

-Tenney Singer (Amazon Review)

REAPING A
SPIRITUAL HARVEST

Rekindle the passion in your devotional life!

Reaping a Spiritual Harvest is a unique devotional tool. The first part contains a study on the biblical principle of sowing and reaping, specifically as it applies to our spiritual lives. The second part of the book contains an interactive 21-page Spiritual Diagnostic Tool. This journaling section comes complete with fill-in-the blanks, scales, question and answers and Scripture passage studies.

The primary purpose of the study is to connect the sowing and reaping process with the spiritual disciplines. Six specific disciplines are considered, including Prayer, Interaction with Scripture, Fasting, Worship, Financial Stewardship and Evangelism. Each discipline has worksheet pages with Examine, Envision and Engage sections to help believers discover their strengths and weaknesses in each discipline and make practical changes to engage with these spiritual disciplines more effectively.

WWW.MAKEWAYMINISTRIES.COM

AVAILABLE IN PAPER AND DIGITAL FORMAT!

Connect with us

 www.makewayministries.com

 Facebook.com/makewayministries

 YouTube.com/makewayministries

 @makewaymin

 @make_way_ministries

 contact@makewayministries.com

www.ingramcontent.com/pod-product-compliance
Lightning Source LLC
Chambersburg PA
CBHW060126130626
46556CB00006B/2251